# Changing
# the Essence

Richard Beckhard

Wendy Pritchard

# Changing the Essence

*The Art of
Creating and Leading
Fundamental Change
in Organizations*

Jossey-Bass Publishers · San Francisco

For sales outside the United States contact Maxwell Macmillan International Publishing Group, 866 Third Avenue, New York, New York 10022

Printed on acid-free paper and manufactured in the United States of America

### Library of Congress Cataloging-in-Publication Data

Beckhard, Richard, date.
    Changing the essence : the art of creating and leading fundamental change in organizations / Richard Beckhard, Wendy Pritchard.
       p.   cm. — (A joint publication in the Jossey-Bass management series, the Jossey-Bass nonprofit sector series, and the Jossey-Bass public administration series.)
    Includes bibliographical references and index.
    ISBN 1-55542-412-0
    1. Organizational change. I. Pritchard, Wendy, date.
II. Title. III. Series: Jossey-Bass management series. IV. Series: Jossey-Bass nonprofit sector series. V. Series: Jossey-Bass public administration series.
HD58.8.B397   1991
658.4'06—dc20                       91-37204
                                                  CIP

FIRST EDITION
*HB Printing*   10  9  8  7  6  5  4  3  2  1                *Code 9218*

*A joint publication in*
The Jossey-Bass Management Series
The Jossey-Bass
Nonprofit Sector Series
*and*
The Jossey-Bass
Public Administration Series

Consulting Editors
Organizations and Management

Warren Bennis
*University of Southern California*

Richard O. Mason
*Southern Methodist University*

Ian I. Mitroff
*University of Southern California*

# Contents

ix

# Preface

## The Growth of This Book

The seeds for this book are in the authors' forty years of combined experience in working with leaders of private and public organizations and institutions who are grappling with the dilemma of managing both the short-term effectiveness and the long-term health of their institutions. It is our belief that those who guide the destinies of our business and public organizations are now facing an unprecedented set of demands and dilemmas. The fertilization of these seeds was the identification by our colleagues and clients of the need for a systematic inquiry into the nature of managing large, fundamental change in complex organizations and the most important issues involved in these changes.

*Changing the Essence* is an attempt to fill that need. We hope that it will also help in the search for ways to manage the tensions that occur between dealing with short-term urgent pressures and addressing the strategic management of organizations' identities and destinies. Significant leadership energy is required to get the balance right.

In the past few years, many organization theorists and writers have paid increasing attention to leadership as a basic factor in the fully functioning organization. Much attention has also been paid to the impact of the organization's culture on its performance and potential. A third subject receiving increased attention is the management of change. Each of these valuable contributions focuses on one aspect of the three interdependent factors: leadership, culture, and change. Their objective is to help the reader understand the factor and its implications for managerial action.

*Changing the Essence,* whose theme is making and managing fundamental change, presents an integrated approach to these three factors. We look at the implications of change for leadership behavior and at ways to create an appropriate organizational culture for achieving change. Most of the illustrative examples in this book are taken from business organizations. We believe, however, that much of what we say in the book applies to both private and public sector organizations, so we refer simply to "organizations" throughout the book.

We hope to help the reader to a better understanding of the conditions that demand a fundamental change strategy and of the power of a vision-driven, integrated approach to achieve this end. We want the reader to understand the need to operate in a "learning mode" that values results and improvement equally. In addition, we would like the reader to have clearer options and criteria for deciding whether the change can and should be managed through present structures and systems or whether a dedicated structure is required to manage the change effort.

We also want the reader to be aware of, and have some tools for managing, the various organizational processes that are vulnerable to change in a fundamental change effort. Finally, we want the reader to have increased access to both the knowledge and skill base that are available to help in managing the change process.

## Intended Audience

Those who have the ultimate responsibility for guiding their organizations into the next century are the primary target for this book. Consultants and experts who advise our primary readership and help them with their choices may also find it useful. For those who study the phenomena of leadership and the management of complexity, diversity, and change, here is another building block in the edifice.

In addition, this book is for us, the authors. For several

years we have wanted to collaborate on a project that could express "who we are" professionally. This book, a guide to creating and managing fundamental change, is the realization of that wish.

## Overview of the Contents

In Chapter One we look at the forces that require leaders to decide to implement a fundamental change. We explore what is involved in choosing a fundamental change strategy, paying attention to diagnostic processes and to the factors that must be considered in the development of an integrated change effort.

In Chapter Two, we focus on our bias toward a basic condition needed in a viable change effort; namely, operating in a learning mode, which demands that equal attention be paid to results and to improvement. We also explore the implications of this mode for leadership behavior, managerial behavior, changes in roles and relationships, and changes to organizational systems and practices such as information systems and rewards.

Chapter Three explores our belief in the necessity for a vision-driven strategy for change and looks at the development of vision by top management. The creation of a process to obtain appropriate commitment throughout the organization is explored, as is an integrated approach to achieving subgoals of the vision. We also look at the management process in the organization to understand how it realizes the vision and sets improvement goals.

In Chapter Four, we focus on five generic themes. These are changes in (1) mission or purpose, (2) identity, (3) relationships to key constituencies, (4) ways of work, and (5) culture. Although all of these themes would be present in any fundamental change effort, the challenge for leaders is to choose one as a driver for the change. We look at them independently in this chapter.

Chapter Five focuses on leaders as participants in fundamental change, on the role they might play, the way they might behave and be seen to behave, and the dilemmas they have to resolve in leading change. In Chapter Six, the theme of "everything changes" is used to explore the multitude of organizational changes that arise from fundamental change, and the way organizations manage their interrelationships to align the change effort. These smaller organizational changes are both part of, and consequent upon, a decision to undertake a fundamental change.

Chapter Seven focuses on the critical factors that require top leadership action to manage the processes of the transition state, where all change occurs. These are managing work and activities, developing strategies and plans for securing commitment from key players, designing communications strategies and programs, and recruiting and using dedicated expertise.

In Chapter Eight, the Epilogue, we look at conditions in the next decade that will require organizations to change their core and essence. We examine the character of the thriving organization that is successfully meeting similar challenges. Finally, we present a profile of the winning leadership that will enable organizations to realize fully their ideal future.

A paradox of today's world is the increasing need for leadership to become involved with creating an organization that is actively moving toward its potential, while at the same time solving today's crisis or emergency. Since often the "urgent drives out the important," the organizational "becoming" is forced to wait its turn. It is the contention of this book that organizations wishing to be top competitors in the years ahead must move the effort "to become" to the head of the line.

## Acknowledgments

We wish to thank the friends and clients whose concern with the subject of change and organizational development has inspired us to take on this project. We thank those who have encouraged us, our colleagues and fellow students of organization. Some family and special friends have invested energy in giving us helpful advice and support: Sandra Barty Beckhard, David Erdal, Brian Inglis, Lois Love, Greg Parston, Daphne Pritchard, Peter Pritchard, George Raymond, and Dorothy Wedderburn.

Several chief executives who have personally led massive change efforts kindly agreed to read the book and provide comments. We are very grateful for their perspectives. Our thanks go to Alex Hart, chief executive officer of MasterCard International; Sir John Harvey-Jones and Sir Denys Henderson, the former and present chairmen of Imperial Chemical Industries; Frances Hesselbein, president of the Peter Drucker Foundation; Duncan Nichol, chief executive of the National Health Service; John Pepper, president of the Procter & Gamble Company; and Harald Norvik, president and chief executive of Statoil.

Our thanks to our editor William Hicks, who from the beginning had faith in us and in the book, and who provided support, criticism, and help throughout. Particular thanks to Tarnia de Val and Diana Turner, who typed, retyped, and organized the manuscript and helped to bring the book to light.

*December 1991*
Richard Beckhard
*New York, New York*

Wendy Pritchard
*London, England*

# The Authors

**Richard Beckhard** has been involved with the management of change for more years than he cares to describe. As one of the founders of the field of organization development (OD), he helped define it as an area of study and practice.

Beckhard consults with the chief executives, boards, and senior managers of organizations in both the private and public sectors. Some of his long-time business clients are Imperial Chemical Industries, Norsk Hydro, the Procter & Gamble Company, and The Royal Bank of Canada. He was professor of organization behavior and management at the Sloan School, Massachusetts Institute of Technology, from 1963 to 1984. At his retirement, the Sloan School honored him with the creation of the Richard Beckhard Prize, given annually for the best article in this area in the *Sloan Management Review*.

Beckhard's books include *The Fact-Finding Conference* (1953), *Core Content* (1956), *Organization Development* (1969), *Organization Transitions* (1977, with R. Harris; 2nd edition 1987), and *Explorations on the Teaching and Learning of Managing Large System Change* (1978). He has written numerous articles in the field of change management. With Warren Bennis and Edgar Schein, Beckhard created the Addison-Wesley Organization Development Series, which currently numbers over thirty books and is generally accepted as the state-of-the-art source.

**Wendy Pritchard** is an occupational psychologist with twenty years of experience in the field of organizational effectiveness and the management of complex change.

She worked for Rank Xerox (UK) from 1969 to 1974, heading up a team of behavioral scientists, and for Shell International Petroleum Company from 1974 to 1989, where she was responsible for providing consultancy to corporate functions and to Shell operating companies worldwide. Pritchard then joined Wolff Olins as board director and now runs her own consulting practice from London. She works with top management in both the public and private sectors.

# Changing
# the Essence

# 1

## Choosing the
## Fundamental Change Strategy

### Forces Requiring Fundamental Change

The world in which we live and will live, and the environment in which organizations will operate, are without precedent. Although the elements are the same, the pace and complexity of changes to new forms, ways of living, and values are of an order of magnitude never before experienced. Changes in the political landscape and new relationships between the First World and the Third World are redefining the marketplace, the means of production, and the location of human, financial, and technical resources.

The explosion of technology in communications and information have indeed created one world in which transactions take a microsecond, and news travels as fast as it can be reported. Worldwide changes in social values, such as concern for the environment, the role of women in society, and the role of wealth-producing organizations, all define the environment in which organizations function.

This environment is making unprecedented demands on organizational leaders, who have the task and responsibility of determining both the functioning and the future of their organizations. This "white water" turbulence is forcing most leaders to examine the very essence of their organizations—their basic purposes, their identities, and their relationships with customers, competitors, and suppliers.

1

The assumptions that guided organizations in the past were (1) that they could control their own destinies and (2) that they operated in a relatively stable and predictable environment. These assumptions are challenged in today's world by, for example, the vulnerability of even the largest organizations to takeovers and recession, the changing nature of industries, and the increased concern with social issues such as protecting the physical environment.

To respond effectively to these demands, chief executives must rethink their own priorities and behavior. Competitive supremacy will be a function not only of increased profits and performance, but of the organization's capacity to innovate, learn, respond quickly, and design the appropriate infrastructure to meet demands and to have maximum control over its own destiny.

For this to occur, top leaders will need to reduce their personal "hands-on" involvement in current operations and replace it with management systems and structures. Leaders must focus on taking the organization into the future. This means developing a vision of the desired future state of the enterprise, creating management structures and systems to achieve this state, and providing personal leadership in directing the process of managing the dynamics of both the organization and its interfaces with its environment.

The management journalist Christopher Lorenz wrote in a recent *London Financial Times* article (Lorenz, 1991): "Under relentless pressure from competitors and costs, and egged on by management gurus such as Tom Peters who preach that 'the only constant thing today is change,' virtually every self-respecting large European and American company these days is running at least one 'organization-wide change programme.' . . . Many of these ambitious, but varied, efforts will either fail entirely, or have a short-term impact and then die. For the management of change is a much more challenging and multi-faceted process than most companies realize."

It is our conviction that for a change effort to move an organization into the future, the process (see Figure 1.1) must involve an understanding of the outside forces that require busi-

Figure 1.1. Fundamental Change Model.

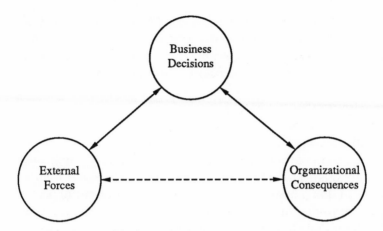

ness decisions for change, such as going global, becoming customer driven rather than technology driven, or becoming service oriented rather than product focused. All these kinds of business decisions have such profound consequences for the organization that the essence of the organization must change. The topic of this book is the creation and leadership of changes to the essence of organizations, a process that we have called *fundamental change*.

## Choosing a Fundamental Change Strategy

In considering the forces for change, the business decisions to be made, and their organizational consequences, leaders need to choose between treating the change in an incremental and linear way or in a fundamental, systems-based, and diagnostic way.

    If an incremental change strategy is chosen, it is likely to deal with "first things first" and to make the necessary changes in sequential order. If a fundamental change strategy is chosen, the implications for the organization are that the organization itself, its parts, and their relationships will simultaneously change. The subparts of the organization must be committed to change and have action plans in place that fit the constellation of changes needed and that are aligned with the leaders' vision of an end state.

*Characteristics of a Fundamental Change Strategy*

The leaders of the organization must have a clear vision of the desired end state of the entire system, including such dimensions as its business, its organization, and its ways of working. This vision must be used as a common context both for diagnosing the need for changes and for managing the process of change, so that it acts as an integrating force for the multitude of apparently disparate changes to be made. The plan for making the changes must be an integrated one.

An integral part of a fundamental change strategy must be a conscious decision to move to a learning mode, where both learning and doing are equally valued. This is an essential precondition for managing fundamental change effectively and is also a fundamental change in its own right. A further essential ingredient is a clear commitment by top leaders to making a significant personal investment in developing and building commitment to an inspirational vision, and to examining and using their own time and behavior in ways that are congruent with this vision.

Many leaders have responded to outside forces by developing an immediate action plan to effect changes. It is not "natural" for dynamic leaders to respond to pressures by saying, "Let's stop and look at where we want to be, let's see how that is different from where we are now, and let's make a plan to get there."

---

### A Shift from an Incremental to a Fundamental Change Strategy

A chief executive officer (CEO) of a multibillion-dollar financial organization doing business worldwide was discussing with one of us some deep concerns about business strategy. His "products" were almost identical to those of key competitors. He was concerned that his company was losing market share in several markets as a result of a number of factors, including:

- Aggressive marketing strategies and practices of competitors

- Customer resistance to changing buying habits
- Lack of organizational capacity to respond quickly to changes in the business environment
- Inconsistency in management philosophy and practices among top managers around the world

The organization had been developed through a series of mergers with other companies and therefore it had a patchwork culture. The organizational design, a country-based central management, was organized around the creation of financial products and the development and installation of the systems needed to support their delivery. The products were issued by financial institutions.

The chief executive had concluded that to penetrate other markets effectively, the design of the organization would have to change from one centrally directed organization to strong, highly autonomous regional organizations. The central management would resemble a holding company and would be required to develop partnerships with regional management.

From his analysis of the change needed, the CEO had posed the following urgent questions:

- How should authority be distributed between regional managements and the center?
- How should policies such as pricing and marketing strategy be determined?
- How should authority be divided between central staff functions that created products and the decision to use them?
- What impact would structural change have on information management, financial management, and human resource policies?

To respond to these questions, he and his colleagues had developed a strategy. The first step was to appoint and brief the regional executives, then to establish local headquarters and divide roles and responsibilities. Management would determine policies affecting the adoption and use of products by the regions, while at the same time producing a new information management system to ensure that information requirements were successfully met.

To implement this strategy, the management group had developed a timetable that would put regional executives in place within three months, with the rest following as soon as possible.

After describing the change strategy and plan, the CEO paused and reflected that he still had an uneasy feeling that something was not quite right about management's thinking and plans. How quickly could he expect this change to have positive effects on the business? How would he measure success?

The consultant with whom he was working raised a series of questions:

- Did the CEO have a clear vision of what the company would look like in five years' time? What businesses would it be in? Where would it be and how would it be positioned?
- If he had such a vision, was it known, understood, and supported by key staff?
- Had he done an analysis of what would have to be changed to move the organization from its present state to its envisaged state?
- Had he explored the interrelationships between the questions he himself had raised?
- What were the benefits of a region acting autonomously and owning its own resources compared to those of a centrally managed information resource?
- What was the relationship between the staff function of creating products and the regional authority to determine appropriate products?
- Should the basic relationship between regions and the center be that of financial borrower and lender or that of an independent business joined in a network with a central executive?

After considerable thought and discussion, the CEO declared that he felt it was necessary to rethink the situation. He would have to go "back to the drawing board" with his senior colleagues and produce a vision statement that clearly defined what the business and organization should look like in three years. Using this vision, the management group would be able to look at what in the organization needed changing and what interrelationships, policies, and systems would have to be developed.

He also decided that he and his senior colleagues would have to develop a dedicated structure to manage these changes. He accepted that this structure would not be the same as the structure for managing the day-to-day operations.

---

In this example, the CEO's main insight was that an incremental change strategy based on action and reaction would not produce the results he wanted over time. What he needed was a more diagnostic approach to the constellation of issues that was involved and an integrated plan to move the organization where he wanted it to be.

He had recognized that there was a relationship between outside pressures (poor competitive position and market share) and his business response (a more aggressive business strategy), as well as a need for some organizational changes (regionalizing to carry out the business strategy), but had approached these elements in a linear, incremental way rather than looking at them as an integrated whole. What he had not realized was the importance of considering the organizational consequences of his business decision as much more complex clusters of changes.

His *revised* plan was, first, to recognize his personal responsibility to look at a "whole-picture" view of the relationships and connections between the outside demand for change and what the business needed to become. This would be the context for his business decisions and organizational change strategy. He also realized that he needed to establish an integrated way to manage the process of making the changes effectively.

## Diagnosing Changes

The first step in the process of mounting fundamental change is an adequate diagnosis. This involves an analysis of the present reality, including the demands of the environment and the organization's capacity to respond to these demands, and the development of a clear vision of the changed state after the change effort has taken place.

We believe that this diagnostic approach is better than an action approach in managing fundamental change; that is, the vision is used as a guide to determining what should change, rather than today's presenting symptoms being triggers for action.

## Designing an Integrated Management Strategy

A change of this magnitude cannot be described as a single change; in reality it is a constellation of changes that are both discrete and interdependent and that must be managed simultaneously. Success in managing fundamental change includes moving the organization to a mode in which learning and improving the quality of performance are equally valued. The next chapter explores this in more detail.

# 2

■

# Creating a Learning Organization: Balanced Rewards for Results and Improvement

### Making a Conscious Effort
### to Move to a Learning Mode

Readers will be well aware that increasing numbers of organizations all over the world are engaged in massive change efforts, which are designed to improve their competitive position, maintain their present ownership and financial structure, and ensure their future. Many of these efforts will either fail or be short-lived because the leadership is unaware of or does not pay attention to the complexity of the processes involved in such changes.

Probably the most important single process involved in effective change is the process of *learning while doing.* The complexity of change strategies demands that processes of feedback and replanning make up the essential core of change management. In a military campaign, it is a basic principle that intelligence gathering goes hand in hand with delivery. Learning to improve the effectiveness of the effort is a natural component of all strategies and tactics. Yet in many business organizations, executives have trouble applying this principle to the management of the organization. Historic practices, early training, "traditional" values about what are good and bad managerial

9

practices, all combine to reward behavior that is "result oriented" rather than "learning oriented."

However, if the huge changes now under way in the world's major corporations are to be effective, there must be a fundamental change in these attitudes and values. Learning must be seen as not just desirable, but essential to achieving positive change objectives. We are personally familiar with these massive efforts in consumer organizations including Kraft, Pepsico, and the Procter & Gamble Company. Similar changes are under way in British Petroleum, Imperial Chemical Industries, Norsk Hydro, and British Airways, to name a few.

In each of these cases there is a well-thought-out, extensive *change plan*. There is a process for determining the desired state and the major changes in policy and practices necessary to reach it. However, frequently the *implementation plan* is not as well thought out and the change effort is managed through the normal operational hierarchy rather than through a dedicated change management resource. In addition, only a very few organizations have a conscious strategy to implement the plan in a *learning mode*. Normally, change is measured only in terms of results; rarely is there any measurement of the *process* of improvement.

Unless the managements of these organizations reexamine their strategies to include a learning process as an inherent part of their planning and administration of change, they are unlikely to be fully effective or to reap the benefits of accelerating change that a learning mode can bring.

---

### An Action Strategy in a Learning Mode

In 1989, the executive management of Norsk Hydro, a multibillion-dollar industrial group with headquarters in Norway, undertook a massive goal-setting and reorganization exercise in order to assure a successful position at the turn of the century.

Under the title "Hydro 2000," a process was initiated for identifying key issues facing the company. Task forces and inquiry groups were formed that met and made recommendations to the top management concerning goals, strategies, and structures for the coming years.

These efforts resulted in a redefined business strategy and priorities, a statement of Norsk Hydro's business philosophy, and a set of key strategic principles, from which emerged some major business and organizational restructuring. The number of divisions was sharply reduced, with divisions combined into a few business groups. The heads of these new businesses were given much more authority and freedom than had existed before. Each chief executive of a business group would respond to the executive team on matters of strategy and budget and would have a special relationship with one of the executive team members, who would function as a "friend" and as a liaison with the top team.

In addition, for each business a "board" would be created (some of these already existed in the old structure). The board would be chaired by the "friend" from the executive team. Its members would include the chief financial officer and chief executives from other businesses and/or key central staff heads.

So far so good. There was a well-thought-out basic plan; values, philosophy, and principles were clearly stated; and organizational restructuring was set up to carry out the basic plan. The top leadership was prepared to install this new structure and start it working. Information about the specific functions, tasks, and authority of these boards would be developed soon by the executive team or the executive team member who headed a board. The financial controls that would be needed from the center would be determined by the chief financial officer. It was assumed that since the membership of the boards was composed entirely of experienced senior executives, they would know how to behave in their roles as board members.

A final review of the plan was held before it was announced publicly and a starting date determined. At this review, the CEO and some staff members raised the following questions:

- Exactly what was to be the new role of the executive team? Which decisions would it keep as reserved powers and which business board decisions would it review, if any? How would control processes be established and monitored?
- What decisions, if any, would the businesses' boards make? Were they truly boards, or would they act as advisory groups to the chief executive of the business?
- What would be the relationship of the chief executive to this board? What decisions would the chief executive make, with or without approval? Who would be responsible for hiring and firing? Who would decide on capital investments?
- What would be the relationship of the chief executive to the executive team? Would communication take place through the board or independently?
- Would all members of the business board be equal? Or would they perform an advisory function to the executive team member who chairs the board?

As a result of this review, the executive team realized that it had to change its approach and behavior. First, the members had to think through the answers to these questions. Second, they had to recognize that these answers were dynamic and would need to be reviewed continuously as experience developed. They realized that the actual behavior of the executive team might be different in different business areas.

The team members knew that they could not expect instant appropriate behavior from the board members, and that they might be producing more aggravation than help for the chief executives of the businesses. They realized that freedom for chief executives and control from the center were not absolutes and had to be worked through in specific terms.

Based on these and other insights, they determined to begin the implementation of their plans in a learning mode. In their revised action plan, the executive team would determine the mission and the desired working methods of the boards. It would define authority and the relationships between the boards, the executive team, and each business's chief executive. It would establish the role of the executive team chair for a business, the chief executive's role and functions on the boards, and the ways in which issues of financial control would be handled. The team would also develop the essential company-wide personnel policies that would follow the business board's policies.

After the executive team did this work, it would hold separate meetings with each of the business boards. At these meetings the team members would explain the new missions, roles, and relationships to the business boards. After questions and answers, each business board would immediately convene its first meeting. At this meeting it would clarify its mission, "way of work," agenda, processes, and relationships with the chief executive. If additional issues requiring discussion with the executive team emerged from this meeting, they would be allocated to the chair (executive team member) for follow-up.

Explicitly, at this meeting a review and improvement process would be scheduled. For example, every fifth or sixth meeting of the board would include a review in which the members would look at the past five or six agendas in the following terms: Were they dealing with essential matters? Were there matters they should have been dealing with but weren't? What could they eliminate from future agendas? What about the way they worked? Did everyone participate? What about relationships with the chief executive and the executive team? Were there any new issues to be discussed?

At the previous meeting the executive team would have established a "grand design," for example, "We expect these reviews from the boards every six weeks." The

week after the boards submitted these reviews, the executive team, on which all the board chairs sat, would look
at highlights from the team reviews that needed executive team attention. This process would be a permanent
part of the management of the organization.

---

In this case, the top management of the organization
reviewed and redesigned its strategy before starting the implementation of its change plan. Regretfully, in many other cases,
such a review does not take place, with the consequence that
top management wonders why its well-prepared plan is not being carried out as expected.

## Learning and Change

A learning mode only occurs when an organization's top leaders
understand the process, see learning as something to be valued,
and are prepared to personally commit themselves to it. We now
will look briefly at some of the concepts involved in a learning
mode.

Learning and change processes are part of each other.
Change is a learning process and learning is a change process.
Ultimately underpinning these processes are changes in the way
individuals think and act. The learning process involves:

- "Unfreezing" oneself from currently held beliefs, knowledge,
  or attitudes
- Absorbing new or alternative attitudes and behavior
- "Refreezing" oneself in the new state

The change process similarly involves:

- A present or current state
- A transition state
- A changed state

To move an organization from a result-oriented mode to
a learning mode involves both processes. The desired state must
be identified by the leaders, the present state described, and the

gap between the two understood. An action strategy for closing that gap must be determined, and an implementation plan and structure for managing the transition can then be designed.

Concurrently, leaders must develop a strategy for unfreezing people and groups from existing attitudes and behaviors. They must develop strategies for teaching new behaviors and for refreezing these people and groups in the new condition, which of course includes the continuing ability to learn and improve. All of this requires conscious and explicit planning and managing, a universal process that is described in Chapter Seven. It cannot be left to chance or good intentions.

The most important single instrument for ensuring that learning and change take place is the set of positive and negative rewards that are demonstrated by management behavior. If the stated values and priorities are not consistent with the behavior of the leadership, the change will not stick.

The current management literature is full of articles on the "learning organization." We have selected some readings that should be of interest in the context of managing fundamental change. For example, Arie de Geus (1988) past head of planning for the Royal Dutch Shell Group of Companies, has stated: "This [the learning organization] may be the only sustainable competitive advantage." Ray Stata, CEO of Anolog Devices (in Senge, 1990), makes the same point, as do more and more leaders of high-performing organizations.

Argyris and Schön (1978) have said, "Organizational learning involves the detection and correction of errors," and according to Schein (1985), for change to occur, the organization must "unlearn" previous beliefs, be open to new inputs, and relearn new assumptions and behaviors.

Argyris and Schön (1978) differentiate between what they call "single loop" and "douple loop" learning. In "single loop learning" members respond to changes in the internal and external environments in a way that allows them to maintain the current "theories in use" of ways they think and act. In "double loop learning," error is detected and corrected in ways that involve modification of an organization's underlying norms, policies, and objectives. This concept is comparable with the distinction between incremental and fundamental change.

An effective change strategy would be one that takes account of the organization's memories, maps, norms, and values. The normal "cascade" strategy for implementing change is usually ineffective, because memories remain embedded in the way the organization works after the change. This applies particularly if the change relates to the culture rather than to work practices or systems.

One characteristic of a true learning organization is that the norms encourage innovation. Another is that problems are approached in an integrative way. Kanter (1983) expresses this well by describing the ability "to see the whole as opposed to parts and challenge the established patterns rather than walling off a piece of experience."

Leaders play a crucial role in moving an organization toward a learning mode, as they do in managing all fundamental change. What particular aspects of their actions and their influence on others are relevant to developing a learning organization?

## Behavior and Commitment in Top Management

### *"Putting Your Behavior Where Your Money Is"*

As we have said, the most critical factor in moving to a learning mode is the behavior of leadership and management. In the Norsk Hydro case, top management was committed to this process and changed its method of management to include explicit learning goals. However, this occurred in a culture where middle management did not share in the learning approach. People were used to a culture in which each level of the organization was clear about its function and authority, whereas the process initiated by top management moved control of the destiny of some parts of the organization to the people who were the direct leaders of those areas.

The apparent desirability of change, and the enthusiasm for its implementation that is felt by top management, may not generate enthusiasm down the line, but may instead produce aggravation and lack of enthusiasm. Top management has been through a learning process, but it may not have created an equivalent process for those lower in the hierarchy.

An example of this is given in the story of a senior executive in a large global company that had undertaken a major culture change effort.

---

The executive called one of us primarily to express her frustration at what was happening. The company's top management had enthusiastically embraced both the plan and the process of this major change effort.

To implement the plan, various committees were established, including a top management group that was to function as a steering committee and a behavior model. In its function as a steering committee, it controlled the speed of change as well as the financial aspects.

The frustration the caller reported was that the top group, although it encouraged and espoused the change, was in fact holding on to old traditions, "memories," and successful past work patterns and methods. Members of middle management were complaining, particularly in regard to innovation. They said, "You ask and encourage us to work in new ways. What are you doing yourselves? How can you behave in ways that will free us up to follow our energy and ideas, rather than feeling that old punishments will apply?"

Top management had not built in a learning mode; therefore, the frustration felt by middle management was only expressed to top management by the corporate staff, people who did not have first-hand knowledge of the middle-level feelings. If it were expressed by the line, it would be considered "feedback"—meaning negative input. Top management realized the effects of its own behavior and developed a process of joint periodic meetings between levels with the explicit agenda of examining learning that resulted from the change effort and designing a program for improvement.

---

*Personal Commitment by Leaders*

A learning mode can only become part of the basic culture of the organization if members of the top and senior management are personally committed to making the organization operate in this way. This means that top management must act to align its behavior with its stated commitment. Members need to become more aware of the signals they give to the organization through their behavior, whether these signals are the ones they want to give, and whether they match the desired changes.

*Enrolling the Commitment of Other Key Players*

Another key aspect of top management's behavior in moving toward a learning mode is its interaction with key line and staff subordinates. To implement an extensive change of culture, it is not enough for the chief executive to make public appearances to support the change. He or she must also display congruent behavior in relationships with immediate colleagues. Some members of management will consciously or unconsciously resist a change until they have identified with it and made it their own. What leaders discuss in performance reviews sends strong messages about their true beliefs. Reviewing business and organizational objectives in order to be certain that there is a learning component will help the perception of consistency. However, holding colleagues accountable for behavior that supports both the change effort and learning objectives may require more attention than a leader would ordinarily pay to such matters.

## Implications for Related Changes

*Rewards That Match Learning Behavior*

Leaders must express their commitment by developing an integrated system for performance reviews, improvement reviews, and the attachment of compensation to these reviews.

Reward systems must support the learning stance. This implies that bonuses are given in some balance between performance and improvement or learning. As with all changes, this may meet with resistance, which top management must overcome in order to align rewards with values and priorities.

## Management of Information

Different types of information are needed with a learning mode. Top management is responsible for setting up an information management system to ensure that appropriate information is available where it is needed. Beyond the information department, changes may be made to procedures, reporting, policy design, and the details of the way people work, for example, by incorporating voice mail or video conferencing.

One of the crucial factors in becoming a learning organization is feedback, which is a prerequisite in the learning process. The flow of information and the technology required to help this process must be designed with the aim of quickly sending appropriate information about their performance to individuals and groups so that they can not only learn but accelerate their improvement.

## The Strategic Planning Process

Leaders must examine their strategic planning process. Key executives and planners should regard the planning process as organizational learning (Watson and Pritchard, 1985). Through the planning process, they can show what the organization has learned about itself and how it may be improved.

The planning process is a powerful tool for helping individuals and the organization learn from the past and for projecting this learning forward in a mind-set oriented toward the future.

## Education and Training

Many large, modern organizations clearly support learning by investing significant money in management development and education. For example, IBM requires every person to spend two weeks each year learning. In these types of organizations, personnel policies support employees and encourage them to improve in their jobs, as well as creating opportunities for personal and professional growth.

In the fundamental change toward becoming a learning organization, the role of management development and education is to ensure that all curricula include attention to learning and improvement as well as to performance and results. Leaders must direct their management development efforts toward becoming a key lever in the creation of a learning organization. The Norsk Hydro case exemplifies both the more traditional approach to leading massive change and the strategy that incorporates managing in a learning mode as a basic part of the effort.

We now look at a case in which an organization consciously determined from the outset to move to a learning mode. The primary force for change was a loss of market share. The organizational consequences of the business decision to recapture this share included the development of a vision to move the organization to a different place and the creation of a plan to implement the vision.

---

### Moving Toward a Learning Culture

For many years, the Xerox Corporation maintained a commanding position in the office machine business. In recent years, however, new developments at the Eastman Kodak Company, NEC Corporation, and other companies had made competition in the copier field "horrendous." Xerox was losing market share to competitors, and its production of new products was no longer on the leading edge.

Xerox's top management, deeply concerned about this condition, resolved to recapture the market lead. First, they realized that they needed a rallying vision. They created an identity slogan and the chief executive developed an improvement strategy. Divisions and units were asked to prepare short- and medium-term goals and to connect them with the corporate vision.

Although many organizations would have stopped there and waited for the improvements that could be obtained by implementing these goals, the Xerox management chose to apply a more systems-oriented change model by defining its vision as the state it wished to reach. The goals and implementation plans were the activities necessary to reach this state. Top management also realized that the current culture had not produced the level of creativity and innovation necessary to become the leading competitor. The leaders knew that this was not because of a lack of talent, so it must be related to the conditions and environment in which people operated.

With the help of consultants, the chief executive set up a diagnostic process to find an answer. A number of studies were commissioned, with study groups composed of a variety of resources across functions and levels. These groups were given specific questions to address. One study found that there was a major discrepancy between the expectations for performance and the operating "norms" as expressions of corporate values. For instance, one strong cultural value was what they called the "big-hit home run." Success measured against that norm was highly rewarded, whereas small innovations and ideas, and collaborative efforts, were not valued nearly as much. Another norm was that activity was much more valued than learning.

From these studies came the obvious finding that changes were needed in the operating methods, rewards, performance appraisals, and types of information used by top management to monitor these "soft" variables. Cross-functional teams were created and rewarded for team output. Increased attention to learning was supported by procedures that documented learning as well as activities. Rewards were adjusted to relate to both areas.

Perhaps the biggest discovery was that the capacity to learn was critical in Xerox's highly competitive environment. One study team reported a strong association between group and organizational learning, with many small things building on one another. Co-locating groups that can easily associate and build on the little things is directly implied. The analysis also showed a direct parallel between the "big-hit home run" norm and corporate management's beliefs about the importance of control. Moving to the learning mode involved a reexamination and change in those beliefs, which resulted in relocating control, power, and capacity.

Today, Xerox's leadership unhesitatingly connects the change effort with significant improvements in new product innovations and a subsequent increase in market share.

---

### Profile of a Learning Organization

We have been talking about operating in a learning mode in relation to a fundamental or basic organizational change. The most effective organizations we know operate in a learning mode all the time. A value system that emanates from the top and that is widely shared demonstrates that "learning and doing" is a better way to live and work in an organization than just "doing." We look now at some of the characteristics of such an organization.

A learning organization that is functioning well has several elements in place:

- A clear picture of how the organization should operate; employees at all levels understand the importance of both learning and doing.
- Rewards that encourage people to follow these norms. Employees are encouraged and rewarded for asking questions and challenging ways of work, with ideas coming from anywhere. Systems exist that encourage entrepreneurial behavior—as in the 3M Company, whose aligned policy and reward system is described in Chapter Six.
- Performance reviews and career development that look at both what you do and what you have learned; organizations offer compensation systems that support the stated values

and bonuses and incentives that are balanced between current performance, innovation, courage, and risk.

- Feedback systems that guarantee ongoing information, not only about what has been done but about what has been learned that affects future actions. Improvement is valued as much as results. Personal feedback on performance, both positive and negative, is given frequently, up, down, and sideways in the organization.
- Information systems that are designed and managed to support this balance between performing and doing. Information on "lessons" as well as on results should be widely available.
- Training and education programs that are designed to support the change strategies and the values held by top management. If learning is a priority, educational programs should be designed to maximize the balance between learning and doing.
- A communication strategy and program that keeps learning in the forefront of everyone's consciousness.
- A strategic planning process that is thought of as a learning as well as a doing process. More often strategic planning is regarded solely as a way of producing plans to fit the planning cycle. It can, in addition, be a most powerful lever for helping key people to learn, to change their mind-sets, and to develop a future focus.
- Strategic objectives that are defined to include the learning that must take place in order to achieve them.

In a learning organization, the organizational leader will have developed answers to the following types of questions:

- What conditions do we want to have in place when we are in a learning-plus-doing mode?
- What behavior will be expected when learning questions are explicitly added to management and employee actions? What behavior will be rewarded and how will it be measured?
- Who needs to know what the "changed state" will look like? When must they have information?

- What changes in behavior are required from the top? For instance, what should management do in setting up the change strategy and in managing the transitional state? What signals should members of management give with their behavior? What example should they set? What should they manage themselves and what should they set up structures to manage? And which commitment behavior should they follow: to let it happen, to help it happen, or to make it happen?
- What changes in behavior are indicated for senior operating and middle management? Who must be enrolled and committed? What strategy is necessary for obtaining that commitment? How can one reduce natural or situation-induced resistance?
- What changes must take place in the reward system and feedback mechanisms to reinforce and support changes in culture and behavior?
- What changes in the informational system are needed to support the desired behavior?
- What changes in personnel practices such as recruiting, training, and career planning must be made to align them with the strategy?
- What communication systems must be put in place so that people in all parts of the organization will understand and connect their own contributions with the change effort?
- How should the "natural" distrust of such a basic change of emphasis be managed? How do we convince people to believe and be willing to act on new assumptions about learning?
- How do we manage the strong power of organizational memory and traditions? What unfreezing mechanisms are called for?
- What change management structures must be put in place to direct, coordinate, and monitor the total effort?

Because becoming a learning organization is a fundamental change, it follows that once the decision to move to this condition has been taken, everything in the organizational system — people, procedures, and policies — must be reexamined and aligned with the change goals. The next chapter will discuss what it means to lead a vision-driven change effort.

# 3

■
_____

# Leading a Vision-Driven
# Change Effort:
# A Commitment to the Future

### Key Factors in Vision-Driven Change

There are four key aspects to vision-driven change:

- Creating and setting the vision
- Communicating the vision
- Building commitment to the vision
- Organizing people and what they do so that they are aligned to the vision

A vision is a picture of a future state for the organization, a description of what it would like to be a number of years from now. It is a dynamic picture of the organization in the future, as seen by its leadership. It is more than a dream or set of hopes, because top management is demonstrably committed to its realization: it is a *commitment*.

An effective vision will have a consensus among top management over the end state toward which management is moving the organization, and it will need processes for building commitment to it among key managers in the organization. The vision provides a context for designing and managing the change goals and the effort needed to bridge the gap to reach those goals.

Key activities for leaders in directing vision-driven change are:

- Developing a vision and commitment to it
- Ensuring that the vision is communicated clearly to other parts of the organization
- Diagnosing the present condition of the organization on the same dimensions and identifying the gaps
- "Managing the management" of closing the gaps

---

### Creating Culture Change Through a Vision-Driven Process

Statoil, the Norwegian national oil company, was established in 1972 as the "guardian" of Norway's oil and gas resources. By 1990 it had become a company of more than 13,000 people with a turnover of 72,356 million Norwegian Kroner (approximately $10.8 billion). It is changing its identity and culture from being a national exploration and production company to becoming an integrated oil, gas, and petrochemicals company, operating internationally, with its oil and gas reserves putting it in the top group of energy companies.

Harald Norvik was appointed president and CEO in 1988 and led the company in making these changes in identity and culture. He decided that he needed to develop a common vision among his top team in order to guide the entire company in aligning its culture and way of working with its business goals. He thought that the top management group, representing four business areas and the corporate functions, should work together with him on this project. He also declared his intention that Statoil should become a "learning organization," to help it make these changes and to build a basis for future effectiveness.

#### Process for Creating and Setting the Vision

The top management group held a series of offsite meetings over a period of eighteen months. The process started by the creation of a time horizon, for the purposes of the exercise, of the year 2000, with a brainstorming meeting where the leaders put their thoughts together against a "map" (see Figure 3.1).

**Figure 3.1. Change Framework Used by Statoil in Building Its Vision and Identifying Gaps.**

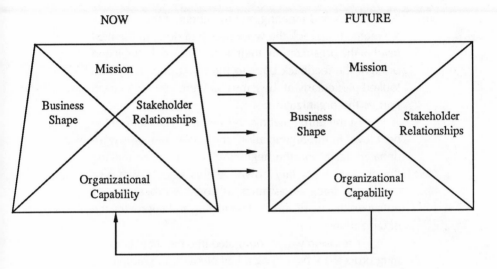

In the first meeting they worked on what form they would like the organization to have in the year 2000, including:

- Their mission and the key words used to describe it
- The shape of their business and the products and markets they hoped to be in
- Their key relationships and what form they would like these to take, for example, with their competitors, their owners, their customers, and their employees

They then thought through the capabilities the organization would need to fulfill these desires. What would it mean to the culture, competences, processes, behavior, structure, and so on?

In the second meeting, the team members refined and selected the output of the first meeting and started to work on identifying the gaps between the reality of today and the picture they had painted of tomorrow.

## Communicating and Building Commitment to the Vision Among Key Managers

After the second meeting, the members of the top management group took the work they had done to the next level of the organization, their teams; they debated it and brought the feedback back to the top group. They also looked particularly at the gaps that were specific to each part of the organization.

At the third meeting, following feedback from the next level in the organization, the vision and gaps were debated again and the beginnings of a plan for making the changes were laid down. At this stage it was also decided to integrate as much as possible processes and initiatives that were aimed at managing and improving the organization.

The vision was incorporated into the strategic planning process by becoming a key element in guiding the choice of strategic options. Assessing the organization's capability early in the determination of strategic options was a further modification of the planning process.

In addition to consultations within the line organizations, a series of organization-wide meetings with key managers involved additional levels of the organization in working on the vision and key gaps and in providing feedback to top management.

## Attention to the Team

During this process the top team members recognized that they were setting themselves a challenging task with their vision, so they also did regular work on their own effectiveness. This included:

- Working on their openness and trust with each other and their ability to give feedback

- Refining their decision-making and problem-solving processes
- Deciding on an appropriate distribution of their time and effort, both personally and as a group (for example, discussing how to shift from an emphasis on managing day-to-day affairs to an emphasis on shaping the future and managing the organization toward the future)
- Balancing the effort and focus between the corporate and divisional roles each of them was playing
- Enlarging their capacity to review and learn from this process as a whole

After much reworking, the vision was regarded as complete enough to publish and communicate. By this time, every word had been carefully studied in the search for common meaning, and each had its particular place.

### Communicating the Vision

A process of communication was set up, initially with the group of key managers who had been involved in developing the vision from the outset, and then with all of the staff. Harald Norvik personally communicated the vision in a series of staff meetings that took place over two months; he was supported at each meeting by members of his top team. This represented a huge amount of top management time, but the investment of this time was regarded as a crucial signal to the organization that demonstrated the importance top management attached to the vision and its implications.

The vision was very well received in the organization. The top managers were aware that it had created expectations and that an appropriate and well-communicated process for realizing the vision was essential.

### Early Steps in Realizing the Vision

Meanwhile, the first step in realizing the vision was under way in a number of different processes and activities.

Top management was eager not to exhaust the organization by setting up yet another special and separate project but rather to enable the new way of thinking and working to become a way of life. This was done in two ways:

1.  By adjusting the organizational processes and the "rules"
2.  By setting guides for the organization through clearly communicated business and organizational improvement priorities, clear values, and principles of managing and acting

A number of interconnected activities are now under way. One is that the vision now directs the organization toward both business goals and organizational goals. Each business area (exploration and production, gas, petrochemicals and plastics, and refining and marketing) is engaged in building its business and organizational strategies for development and will be working on its improvement goals toward the vision.

A start has been made on reviewing jointly in the top managerial group the processes and progress made within each business area, to enable managers to learn from each other and seek synergy of both processes and outcomes. In addition, the strategic planning process has been modified and developed in various ways. The vision was incorporated into the process as a context for assessing strategic options. The two streams of business development and organization development are clearly defined but are seen as parallel (and interconnected) rather than as sequential. Critical success factors for measuring the progress of both business and organization development are being established. A functional network of planners across the organization has been set up to help facilitate the horizontal and learning nature of strategic planning.

The top management group also recognized the importance of and need to develop the human resource role and processes in order to drive the desired changes forward. In particular, the group is discussing the alignment of the appraisal process, the rewards and training required for the new vision and principles, and ways to harness the existing opinion survey of staff as a means of measuring progress.

The top managers have set up a series of meetings to develop and review jointly the corporate values and principles for managing and acting. The meetings include the top management team and other senior managers as participants. The top leaders believe that, as with the vision, it is crucial for these values and principles to be "owned" by the entire senior management. They hope the outcome of these meetings will be a commitment by the organization's leaders to use these principles and values as the guide to their behavior.

After the principles and values are agreed upon, they will be published and distributed throughout the organization, along with a description of the senior managers' actions. The assumption behind this is that if the behavior and attitudes of management are understood, the desired level of commitment throughout the organization will be achieved.

---

This case illustrates a number of points that we have tried to emphasize:

- The leader determined that it was necessary to look at the total picture of the organization in order to help the structure, culture, and way of working to fit well with the business decision to become an integrated international company.
- The eventual vision statement was developed by the top group. This task could not be delegated.
- During the formation of the vision a process was used to communicate and build commitment to it among key managers in the organization, and to give feedback to top management.

- A formal organization-wide communication process visibly led by top management was consciously established once the vision was complete.
- The top management group was patient with the process of building the vision and recognized that this process was important in itself in contributing to commitment and aligning understanding, rather than only being a means of producing a vision statement.
- The top group diagnosed the gaps between the current situation and the vision, using the same dimensions, and used this as a context for setting business and organizational goals, particularly in the four business areas.
- There was a conscious effort to work in a "systems" way. The top managers looked at the whole picture and the connections between its parts in both their diagnosis of the need for change and their chosen approach to integrating the separate ongoing improvement initiatives. They saw these as interconnected contributions to realizing the vision, instead of as a series of improvement projects laid on top of one another.
- Top management recognized the need to continue with the process of realizing the vision, and not stopping with a sigh of relief after the vision was produced and communicated, which is what often happens.
- A learning approach was built into both the strategic planning process and top management's efforts to include a review process as a regular part of its own working style.
- Top management recognized the importance of harnessing and aligning the "horizontal" processes in the organization, for example, strategic planning, human resources, and information management.
- The top team also recognized the importance of being competent and functioning well in order to enable the organization to realize the vision; members invested in improving their individual and team effectiveness.
- The team saw its role in leading the process of building and realizing the vision as a mix of developing and communicating content and steering an organizational process.

## Systems Orientation in Vision-Driven Change

In a systems orientation, organizations are thought of as living complex systems, whose parts exist in a delicate balance with one another, have a common purpose and identity, and are set in a common, changing context.

Systems thinking involves viewing the "world" as a whole composed of many parts that interact with each other in a dynamic way. As in the case of Statoil, the company is a system with many subsystems, all of which are interconnected. Thinking in systems terms means being aware of the web of interrelationships that exist between the parts (or are wanted in the changed state) and being aware of the parts themselves.

Peter Senge, in his book *The Fifth Discipline* (1990, p. 6) describes it dramatically:

> A cloud masses, the sky darkens, leaves twist upwards and we know that it will rain. We also know that after the storm, the runoff will feed into groundwater miles away, and the sky will grow clear by tomorrow.
>
> All these events are different in time and space, yet they are all connected within the same "pattern." Each has an influence on the rest, an influence that is usually hidden from view. You can only understand the system of a rainstorm by contemplating the whole, not any individual part of the pattern.
>
> Business and other human endeavors are also systems. They too are bound by invisible fabrics of interrelated actions, which often take years to fully play out their effects on each other. Since we are part of that lacework ourselves, it is doubly hard to see the whole pattern of change. Instead we tend to focus on snapshots of isolated parts of the system, and wonder why our deepest problems never seem to get solved.

Systems thinking also implies concern for and attention to "connections." In a fundamental change effort the parts are all connected in a dynamic manner. For example, the relationship between product development and manufacturing management cannot be written into a traditional job description. The appropriate behavior depends on the work to be done, interconnections with other parts of the organizations and the outside world, any current acute pressures, and many other factors.

In addition to relationship and role connections, attention must be paid from the outset to the connections between changes in tasks and information system requirements, and between changes in objectives or priorities and changes in rewards. The connections and dissonances between future operating conditions and the present mode must also be addressed.

Managing fundamental change involves looking at the whole organization, its subparts, and the relationships between them. All of these elements will change in fundamental change, and the leaders must diagnose not only what they are now but what form they will take in the changed state, and an integrated plan for change must be devised to bridge the differences.

In developing this plan, it is important for leaders to define both the types of relationships desired for the end state or vision and, separately, the relationships that will be necessary to manage the transitional state, where all the change takes place. Choosing an appropriate change "map" helps top management in addressing and communicating these subjects.

In conclusion, effective vision-driven change using systems thinking involves:

- Having an overall picture of the organization in the future when the change has been completed, and determining how the relationships between the parts of the organization will look
- Obtaining commitment to this picture from key managers
- Using the vision as a common context for developing goals for business and organizational change and improvement
- Understanding the relationships between the culture of the future, the structure of the organization, allocation of work to particular tasks, the information systems, and employees' sense of meaning in working there

We want to underscore at this point the absolute essentiality of a fundamental change effort being vision-driven. The vision of the end state is a statement of leadership's priorities and commitments. It is the expression of the context, within which goals must be set, activities determined, and commitment secured.

Top management alone can define the vision of what the organizations must become. It needs to set up and manage a conscious plan for developing commitment to the vision. As commitment to this vision spreads throughout the organization, new issues arise: How do we get to the desired state? What strategies and programs are needed? How will the implementation effort be conducted? What will be the focus?

In dealing with this last question, leaders need to choose a theme that will be supported and implemented by a critical mass of the organization's leadership and members. This theme will provide the focus for their efforts.

In the next chapter, we identify five general themes, some or all of which are always present in a fundamental change. The challenge for top leadership is to determine which themes provide the best context for the change effort and whether one theme should be dominant, with other themes supporting it. We give examples of how these choices are made and the strategies underlying the choices.

# 4

■

# Focusing the Effort:
# Crucial Themes
# That Drive Change

What underlies fundamental change in addition to its being vision-driven? We have identified five themes that may serve as the focus of fundamental change:

- Change in the mission or "reason to be"
- Change in the identity or outside image
- Change in relationships to key stakeholders
- Change in the way of work
- Change in the culture

Leaders need to think about the themes or foci that describe the change effort being undertaken. For example, if they decide to change their *key relationship* with their suppliers in some way that becomes a fundamental change, all the points we have made about fundamental change will follow. At the same time, other changes will occur that leaders must consider. For example, a change in their relationship with suppliers from "friendly adversary" to "partner" may also require some changes in the *mission* or reason to be, including a change in the public *identity* of the organization or in the basic *way in which work within the organization is done*. It probably will also affect the *culture*. Although one focus of change may lead, others will inevitably follow. All these perspectives are connected, and yet effective change will be facilitated if top management can identify and manage the change with one of these perspectives as a pulling force (see Figure 4.1).

We will look in more detail at each of the five themes, examples of their use, and implications for the management of change.

### Change in the Mission or "Reason to Be"

This theme is the driving force when leadership decides that the "reason to be" or purpose of the organization must be changed. Such a decision then requires subsequent decisions about changes in the way of work, outside image, and organizational design and structure.

Figure 4.1. Focus for Fundamental Change.

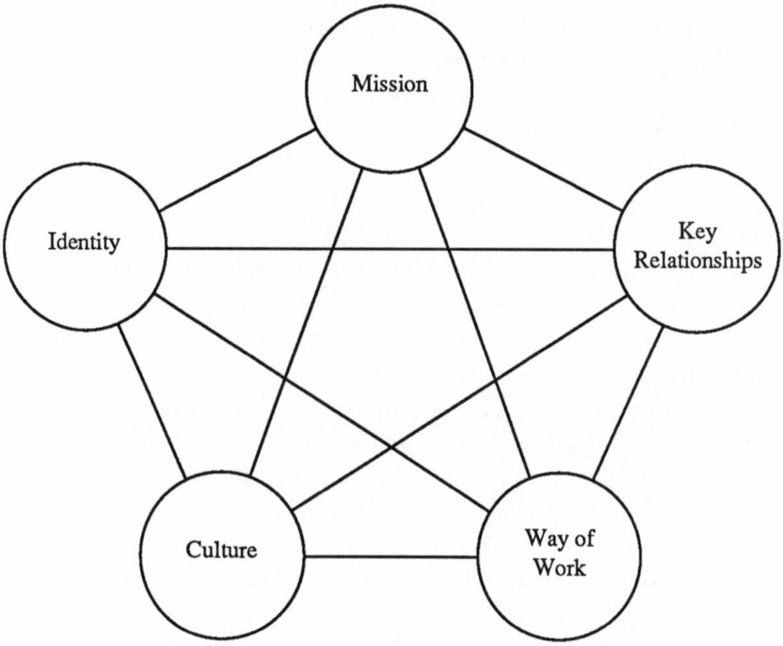

A change in mission resulted when the leaders of Federal Express decided that they were in the transportation business rather than in the package delivery business. In addition to choosing a primary theme—change in mission— they decided that two other themes flowed from this choice: change in the way of work and change in the culture.

To implement these themes, several major changes in functioning were designed and put in place. The leaders of Federal Express changed the basic assumption governing their delivery mechanism. Under the old assumption, their strategy was the same as their competitors': best results were achieved by a delivery system that transported from pickup point to delivery point by the shortest direct route. Under the new assumption, the transportation policies and practices were based on the "hub concept" adopted by many airlines. In this mode, a package was flown from its starting city to a hub city (Memphis, Tennessee, was chosen). All packages from everywhere in the United States arrived in the hub city before 10 P.M., every day. A large staff of handlers (part-time employees, mostly college students) sorted all the incoming materials and redirected them to their final destinations. From 2 A.M. onward, planes left Memphis and flew to these locations for final ground delivery.

In addition to this change, Federal Express developed a new and dedicated information system that allowed the company to have constant real-time information on the whereabouts of every package.

The clear choice by management of the primary theme, and its consequential requirements for action, ensured that the organization would be aligned in its implementation of the decision.

Awareness of the need for a current and clear statement of mission as a part of setting a vision and goals is growing and is causing many large organizations to reexamine their traditional statements for relevance.

## Change in Identity

We propose this as a separate category because it often starts from a different motivation from a change in mission. Changes in mission usually flow from the energy of leaders that is directed toward reexamining and restating the fundamental purpose, whereas identity change usually flows from the need to recoup or regain competitive leadership. It is usually the result of some major outside force or technological breakthrough. Well-documented examples of this are the changes in identity of many financial institutions from "banks" to "financial services" organizations.

---

Sears, Roebuck & Co. is a dramatic example of an organization whose goal was to change its identity from a retail business to a one-stop service, by way of a financial services group. The achievement of that goal had mixed results. We would speculate that part of the reason for its less than fantastic success was that the identity change did not register with the consumer. Most consumers still preferred to think of Sears as a high-quality, low-cost, easily accessible retail company. We would further speculate that the staff members who interacted with customers did not reflect the change, but worked hard to maintain their traditional identity as retailers.

---

A change in identity not only involves outside expressions such as logos, symbols, and advertising strategies. It also involves a well-planned effort to address the attitudes and resistances that are likely to occur in the organization itself. Unless there is visible behavior from the top leaders indicating the importance of implementing this change, it is unlikely that high commitment will occur with members of the organization.

Wally Olins (1989), who has been described as the "doyen" of the corporate identity business, states in the introduction to his recent book *Corporate Identity:* "The identity of the corporation must be so clear that it becomes the yardstick against which its products, behavior and actions are measured." He further states: "It [the book] takes the view that the corporation's actions are indivisible: that how it behaves, what it says, how it treats people, what it makes and sells are part of a single whole."

## Change in Relationships to Key Stakeholders

Most large consumer organizations are reexamining their marketing or selling strategies. They are forced into these examinations by changes in consumer habits, but even more by changes in the purchasing policies and practices of large customers. It is no longer acceptable to have fifteen or twenty salespersons calling on one purchasing department.

---

A large manufacturing company had a history of satisfactory relationships, which could be described as "friendly adversarial," with its suppliers. The leaders of the company decided that if they could change the nature of the relationships to "partnerships," both the company's performance and its competitive position would be improved.

The leadership initiated a program of establishing new arrangements with all of the company's major suppliers. These arrangements were based on the assumption that the company and its suppliers would jointly create new working relationships that would ensure maximum profits for all.

The managers quickly discovered that this program was in effect a fundamental change and that a number of related changes would be required to make it work. For example, changes were required in the functioning of purchasing agents and in the relationship between purchasing and product management. The criteria for "high performance" needed to be revised. New personnel and compensation practices had to be developed.

The organization instituted a series of discussions with its major suppliers in which the agenda was an inquiry into the possibility of this different "partner" relationship. Operationally, suppliers and purchasers would collaborate in working out the procedures that would provide the best chance of increasing profit for both organizations—a "win-win" deal.

There was tremendous resistance from many quarters to this change. Some suppliers felt that they would be losing their power in the negotiation. The purchasing agents in the manufacturing organization saw a loss of control over their own work and noticed changed perceptions of their role by other parts of the company. Employees in manufacturing were threatened by the potential new role of the purchasing employees. The top management of the organization had to bring together the managers of the purchasing and manufacturing functions as well as several others to design an internal strategy that would support the new external relationship with the suppliers.

---

The organizational implications of such a change are tremendous. Issues include:

- A change in the role of the purchasing agent
- New information systems co-located in both suppliers' and purchasers' space
- New policies concerning company secrets and openness toward the customer
- Changed accounting practices
- Redesigned relationships between purchasing, manufacturing, and distribution
- The effect on control of all costs by business units

As a result of these changing customer requirements and policies manufacturers are reexamining their purchasing and selling practices. If the organization's leaders are aware of the complexity of this process, they will set up a change management system that will take into account all of the smaller changes mandated by the basic decision.

As companies scramble to increase their competitive edge by implementing these changes, some result-oriented companies are shooting themselves in the foot.

---

In one such case, the management of a large consumer-oriented company misjudged the complexity of outside pressures and devised a change strategy that was incremental rather than fundamental.

The outside impetus was a change in buying policies of several large customers. The customers were dissatisfied with the organization's sales policies, which required that the purchasers deal with a number of salespeople from the company, each selling individual products or product lines. The customers wanted to deal with many fewer salespeople representing significantly larger numbers of products.

This was an industry-wide problem. The company's management was aware that all its competitors were giving high priority to finding an effective organizational response. Management also knew that it had to define the nature of the problem to be solved. It was finally determined that the company's sales practices—and consequently, the sales department—had to be radically reorganized in order to win the competition for best performance and provide highest customer satisfaction.

What management did not recognize was that the problem required rethinking the company's relationships to key customers, and not a change in the sales function. Major changes were required in the internal relationship between sales and product lines and between functional organizations and product organizations. A new information system was needed; compensation practices had to be revised. A fundamental change strategy was required.

> Given the force of the demands and the necessity
> for a basic change in the conduct of business, the leaders'
> definition of the problem and their strategies for dealing
> with it doomed the effort from the start. Had management
> seen this as a systems problem, the issue would have been
> redefined as requiring a major change in the company's
> relationships with one of its key constituencies.

## Change in the Way of Work

In this category we place changes in the way the organization looks and works. The concern here is that the change should be fundamental to the organization. As in any fundamental change, the consequences may affect both the organization and its outside constituencies. However, unlike changes in identity, where what is important is the way the organization is perceived by the world, these changes are aimed at the way the business and the work are organized.

An increasingly common cause of changes in the way of work is a decision to become a global enterprise. Most organizations are country-based, even if they do business in several countries. In recent years, however, many enterprises have changed to a multinational posture, which involves such strategies as manufacturing in low-wage countries or developing regional sales or distribution centers and administrative headquarters.

Moving to a global enterprise is a fundamental change decision that affects the entire organization. New items to be considered include the criteria for location of the global headquarters; the roles, functions, and powers of the central executive; and the worldwide management structure. The relationships and power distribution between product or business heads, territorial heads, and functions will be different. Financial and personnel policies must be reexamined and quite probably changed. This type of force is driving many of the massive change programs we see today. British Petroleum, Imperial Chemical Industries, Norsk Hydro, and Statoil are examples of this phenomenon.

Changes from technology-driven to customer-driven businesses may lead to associated changes in the way of work — for example, in the way the business is governed. If an organization is going global, the role of the board will be different from its role in other types of business. Changes in posture are needed from executive management to strategic management.

A business decision to become a global enterprise, followed by an internal diagnosis, is likely to lead to changes in the way the organization works. A dramatic illustration of this may be given by one of several global companies.

---

The "before-change" condition was one in which the raw materials were acquired by the purchasing function, and both the products and the machinery on which they were made were designed and monitored by the engineering function. The actual manufacture was under the control of the manufacturing function, but the distribution of finished products was the property of the distribution function.

After a diagnosis, the technical management instituted a new concept called "product supply," based on the flow of products from the time they came into the organization until they were on the customers' shelves. The paradigm changed to one process and the subparts, such as purchasing and manufacturing, involved one team rather than four individual functions.

When this change was announced, colossal resistance occurred. The constellation of changes included changes in the relationships between (1) product supply and product business areas, (2) information and product supply and sales, and (3) parts purchasing, manufacturing, and personnel policies and practices. A separate management system was required to manage and integrate all of the changes and the people who had to carry them out.

---

Changes in the way of work are visible and immediate to organization members; therefore, management must be doubly vigilant to see that the changes are managed in a climate where learning is honored and where there is explicit management of the change. Top management's unique role of managing the change effort should be particularly visible in this case.

## Change in the Culture

This is the most subtle theme of the five, in the sense that all changes imply and often mandate a "culture" change. What we are addressing here is the condition that occurs when a change in the culture is the basic goal.

By culture we mean:

- The set of values (what is good or bad) and assumptions (beliefs about human nature) that distinguishes a particular organization from others
- Norms (ground rules for behavior) and artifacts (such as who gets the corner office) that guide actions in the organization

In the case of Xerox, one of the major subgoals was a change in the cultural norms — replacing "big-win" values with improvement and learning.

A commonly *stated* change goal today is to become more customer and/or service oriented. One can watch any two hours of television and see a minimum of three corporate commercials touting this goal for their companies. For this to be achieved in *reality* requires massive changes within the organization in attitudes, behavior, and rewards.

Whatever decision the top management takes, it must have a follow-up change management plan. Resistance to this type of change is usually strong, even if it may be covert. It is important for management to define the specific changes to be implemented in recruiting policies and practices, career planning mechanisms, and financial and other rewards. An explicit communication strategy is needed when such a change takes place.

Even more than other themes, a culture change usually requires the organization to set up supporting educational activities. A current example consists of the changes made in the training and education programs at the General Electric Company to support the position of CEO Jack Welch that a change in the "genetic code" is required to produce a different kind of leader-manager in the future. This position was described by Noel Tichy of the University of Michigan, who took leave from the university to be manager of GE's Management Development Operation from 1985 to 1987 (Tichy, 1989):

> Radically altering the genetic code of a large successful corporation requires revolutionary action. Since 1981 John F. Welch has been struggling to break the company's old genetic code. The code was built around a core set of principles based on growth in sales greater than GNP [gross national product], with many strategic business units relying on financial savvy, meticulous staff work and a domestically focused company. The new genetic code is to build shareholder value in a slow-growth environment through operating competitive advantage with transformational leadership throughout the organization.
>
> Five years of this effort includes downsizing GE by over 100,000 employees, divesting $6 billion and acquiring $13 billion in businesses which moved GE to No. 3 in the United States in market value from No. 10.
>
> To accomplish the quantum change in GE, a new breed of leader was required. These are leaders who can:
>
> 1. Transform the organization, that is creatively destroy and remake an organization round new visions, supported by revamping the social architecture of the organization.
> 2. Develop global product and services strategies. This means changes in product and service design production, distribution and marketing. Leaders must be able to create new forms of

     design teams, make strategic use of sourcing,
     drive world class standards for design, service
     and performance.

3.   Develop strategic alliances.
4.   Global co-ordination and integration. Better
     communication and cultural integration will
     be required.
5.   Global staffing and development. Present sys-
     tems are outmoded and undergoing total re-
     vamping.

These were not just "motherhood" statements. They provided the basis and the context for a massive development and retraining effort for all GE management. They also provided the stimulus for a significant reexamination of policies and practices by managers throughout the GE world.

Practically all fundamental change involves all five of the themes we have been discussing. Each fundamental change has one particular focus, such as change in mission, identity, or way of work. One of the major tasks of leaders is to understand these themes and their relationships and to determine the focus of a particular change effort and ensure that the organization is designed to implement it.

We move now from looking at themes for change to looking inward at the leader as a person, to determine what his or her concerns are.

# 5

■

# Resolving the Leader's
# Personal Dilemmas:
# Style and Behavior

The personal and private dilemmas and choices facing a person in the top leadership position are always present, but they become acute and potent when an organization faces a fundamental reshaping. The leader must confront these personal issues in order to lead the change effort. The choices are usually experienced as a series of tensions that must be addressed. We will refer to them as dilemmas that must be resolved.

If we look at our model in Chapter One, we see that forces in the environment cause leaders to make significant business and strategic decisions that mandate a fundamental organizational change. In the previous chapters we have looked at what has to be done to design and manage change and, more specifically, what leaders must do. We have looked at the need for leaders to understand the environment and the forces pushing for change. We discussed the issues to be considered in choosing a change strategy when a basic change in the essence of an organization is required. We have looked at the leadership implications of moving the organization to a learning mode and have explored the behavioral issues leaders must confront when designing and directing a vision-driven change effort. In Chapter Four, we looked at the themes that represent the foci of the change effort: mission, identity, relationships, way of work, and culture.

In this chapter we move our attention from what leaders *do* to what people in leadership positions should *know* about themselves: their needs and ambitions, and their multiple roles as organizational leaders and individuals. We have found again and again in discussions with those in top leadership positions that most of them are aware of the tensions they face in these roles. We have also noted that many have found it difficult, if not impossible, to discuss or even to face these dilemmas. Given the pressures induced by the requirements of fundamental organizational change, most leaders mobilize all their energy to meet the challenges that are presented. While they are acting to meet these demands, they are simultaneously energized to reflect, become introspective, and worry about themselves.

## Balancing the Demands of Work and Personal Life

It is paradoxical that the greater the pressures that exist to be a forceful leader of organizational strategies, the more the leader as a person tends to be concerned with her or his ambitions, priorities, multiple roles, and values. It is not at all uncommon for leaders to be deeply concerned about their struggle to prioritize their personal efforts as they cope with managing the tensions caused by multiple demands on them as leaders, individuals, partners, and parents.

A few examples of what leaders have told us will illustrate the point.

A professional CEO of a multibillion-dollar global company undergoing massive outside financial and media pressure told us: "This situation really upsets me! On the one hand I'm very angry at the attacks. My adrenalin is up and I'm ready for a good fight. On the other hand, I'm furious, insulted, and hurt by the direct and implied threats to me and my family. I'm really torn about whether to defend my personal image and identity, or whether to ignore that and go all out to meet the business challenges."

Another chief executive, founder of a multibillion-dollar conglomerate, mused sadly:

I have devoted twenty-five years of my life to building this enterprise into a very successful business. Both the business and I, personally, have an excellent reputation as industry leaders in an excellently managed business. I have created an organizational culture that is both achieving and human.

My family has prospered. We enjoy a respected place in our community.

Suddenly, because of some vicious, greedy people among our competitors and some selfish manipulative individuals in the media, we are under such pressure that the enterprise could fall apart. I cannot and will not let that happen. At the same time, I cannot let these attacks on me and my family go unanswered. I must and I will initiate a basic restructuring of the organization to meet the business and organizational challenges. At the same time, I feel sick about what this situation will mean for the enterprise's, my family's, and my personal identity and image. I feel very alone and frustrated at having to decide both the future of the enterprise and the future of my family.

A third person who had recently been made a CEO of a global enterprise said:

Leading this enterprise into the future is the most exciting business challenge I have faced in my whole career. I wake up early every morning with my mind operating at full speed. I can hardly wait to get to the office.

A crazy thing has been happening to me. Quite often as I'm driving to work full of energy, a number of disturbing questions come into my head. I find myself asking, "What does my excitement about the job really mean? Is it really the most important thing in my life? What price am I and my family paying for my commitment to the job

and my personal success?" I know my wife is un-
happy with our present life-style. She's feeling alie-
nated and not fulfilled. She hasn't made too many
overt demands on me yet, but I feel the pressure.
Our home life is relatively tense — much more than
before I started this assignment.

I am really turned on to the business and personal challenges in this job and I see it being both
exciting and fun for some time to come. Yet I find
myself wondering, "Am I doing the right thing?
Should I consider a modification of my family
needs? What would be the consequence of that for
my business career?" It's a bitch of a problem!

Sir John Harvey-Jones, a very powerful and dynamic
business leader, has addressed this dilemma brilliantly in two
recent books. Harvey-Jones is well known as an outstanding
business executive and strategic thinker. He was chairman of
Imperial Chemical Industries (ICI) for five years. Under his
leadership, ICI enjoyed major business and economic growth.
It also had outstanding success in becoming a culture that could
achieve excellent business results and simultaneously be an exciting and challenging workplace.

Recently, after retiring from the company, he was fea-
tured in a highly popular British Broadcasting Corporation series called "The Troubleshooter." In this series he consulted with
a number of organizations on their business and organizational
issues and dilemmas. His personal performance and success in
this role made the series one of the most popular programs on
television — it received the kind of broad attention usually reserved for programs like "Dallas."

In the years immediately following his retirement from
ICI, Harvey-Jones wrote a book on his years of experience as
chairman. The book was entitled *Making It Happen* (Harvey-
Jones, 1988). From the day of its publication, it was outstand-
ingly successful. This book is a fine portrait of a visionary business and organizational leader, pulling his organization into the
future, in both a business and a cultural sense.

More recently, a second book, *Getting It Together* (Harvey-Jones, 1991), has been published. The book is a very powerful personal portrait of this man, including the story of his role as the leader of a giant company for many years. What we really experience in the book is a picture of a man — driven to achievement and success — using his creative brain to keep his organization effective and competitive. We also see a man deeply committed to his family and home, who is convinced that his soul belongs there.

The underlying theme throughout the book is his constant struggle to meet his two powerful and conflicting needs: to be an important, powerful, and successful business leader and to be a central player in his family. The story of Harvey-Jones's struggle with these tensions makes fascinating and engaging reading. Moreover, it epitomizes and dramatically illustrates how the tension between effective job performance and personal living profoundly influences the leader's unique role and contribution in designing and managing fundamental change.

One small but significant quote from *Making It Happen* is appropriate: "There are two aspects of business that obsess me: one is people, the other is change. Without change, nothing is possible. Not to change is a sure sign of imminent extinction."

## Choosing How to Behave and
## Be Seen as a Leader of Change

We turn now to the second set of personal dilemmas faced by organizational leaders in mounting a large change effort. These are the choices concerning personal behavior in the change process. The principal issues are:

- How much will my behavior be driven and controlled by my own personal beliefs, values, and priorities, and how much by my need to stimulate and facilitate the best leadership behavior by those who must design and manage the organization through the change?
- How will I, personally, resolve the tension between the goals

of the change (changes in roles, structures, and so on) and
the need to increase the capability of managers, at all levels,
to simultaneously protect stability and manage change in
their areas of responsibility?

- What managerial role or roles do I wish to play in the effort:
  project manager-director, "chair of the board," court of ap-
  peal, stimulator-facilitator, or consultant?
- What is the personal basis or bias for deciding the preferred
  roles?
- How do I wish to be perceived? What are the appropriate
  archetypes: visionary, entrepreneur, leader/manager, or
  solid business executive?
- Whose perceptions matter: the board of directors, key colleagues and subordinates, competitors, the media, or the
  shareholders?
- What "messages" do I want to send and to whom? (This
  might include statements of goals or visions, strategies, or
  communication with key stakeholders, the board of directors, the media, the stockholders, or the financial analysts.)
- What aspects must I personally manage? (This could include
  working with key subordinates, colleagues, and staff members in filling in the change strategy. It might also include
  one-to-one work with key subordinates to define their roles,
  goals, and commitment to the effort, or it might involve a
  review of the organization's capability to manage the change
  effort. It might also include taking personal control of the
  strategic planning process.)
- How can I manage the management? (What structures, fact-
  finding groups, task forces, or transition management teams
  should I set in place? What new tasks should be assigned
  to operating managers to assure aligned effort in the change?
  What information do I need about the various systems, policies, and practices that must change in order to support the
  basic effort?)

In summary, the decision to undertake a fundamental
change effort has an immediate and profound impact on the
leaders of the organization. In addition to all the executive and

managerial decisions that must be made and implemented, leaders must address profound personal issues. They must examine their business and organizational roles and priorities and think about the effect of the change effort on their personal identity and key relationships. To deal with these demands, they will find it necessary to establish personal priorities. An early priority is the determination of what the leader needs to know and understand about the other changes that result from the fundamental change decision.

# 6

■

# Aligning the Organization: Integration of Roles, Systems, and Rewards

We have discussed earlier the need for an integrated approach when considering fundamental change and the likelihood of all aspects of an organization changing in some way when fundamental change is undertaken. The major difference between fundamental and incremental change efforts is the critical requirement in the former of designing and managing the constellation of changes that flow from the decision to change the essence of an organization.

Once that basic decision has been made, leaders must identify the required changes and develop strategies for designing and integrating them.

- There will be changes in both roles and relationships.
- Changes in human resource policies and practices will be required.
- An information system aligned to the changing conditions will have to be developed.
- Financial management and controls will probably need to be aligned with the new conditions.

We want to examine each of these in more detail.

## Roles and Relationships

As the organization moves toward the new state, senior management needs to redefine its roles, functions, and relationships to other roles. The allocation of decision-making responsibility may need to be changed.

In a change of this magnitude, it is also quite likely that the traditional work of functions such as sales and manufacturing will be replaced by cross-functional teams with group responsibility for outputs. The composition of such teams will probably blur the traditional line/staff role distinction. Work will be more task-focused than role-focused. The designation of performer/supporter roles will replace line/staff roles. This will demand major changes in the functioning of staff.

Top management will need to redesign both the work and the organization structure in ways that require cooperative effort and the elimination of behavior such as protecting one's department or "turf."

## Human Resource Policies and Practices

To implement the basic change decision, it will be necessary to align these policies with the new culture:

- *Performance reviews* will have to be redesigned to apportion rewards between business results for the organization, improvement in the capacities and capabilities of the unit, and personal development goals and results for the individual.
- *Recruiting* may need to be drastically revised. Who does the recruiting as well as the type of contract with job candidates may both change.
- *Compensation policies and systems* must all be examined. For example, will there be one compensation policy for the whole organization or custom-built ones for each business area?
- *Career planning and manpower planning systems* may require alteration.

We have alluded several times to the effect of fundamental change on an individual's job satisfaction and career plans.

It is important that the organization's systems are designed to increase the positive aspects of both.

The human resource management staff has a pivotal role to play both in designing and implementing these changes. The human resource function is the most likely repository for the values of the organization. It is the organization's conscience. Human resource management should take active leadership in aligning the people management practices with the leaders' values and beliefs. In order to do this effectively, the human resource manager must be a full member of the top management team and its spokesperson in the people area.

## Information Management

It will come as no surprise to our readers that the majority of organizational leaders are convinced that information management is the most important factor in organizational performance and competitive advantage. It is increasingly obvious that information management is too central to be controlled by information managers. Decisions about information networks and other uses of exploding technology are top management's responsibility today. But if top management is making these decisions, what is the role of the information division?

The information staff of the future — and, in many cases, the present — will have a number of critical responsibilities. It will house the technical expertise, act as the liaison with the expanding scientific and technological applications, provide leadership in developing relevant applications to present to top management, and continue to provide the support systems needed to effect major organizational decisions.

Four examples may explain these roles more fully.

---

In the mid eighties the leadership of Citicorp recognized that through the introduction of a common computer system throughout the world, it would be possible to process loans days faster than the current practice of international banks allowed.

The information specialists analyzed the various systems in use around the world, selected the most effective one, and set about installing it worldwide. Little did they realize that they had instituted a fundamental change! This technical change came up against massive resistance in various countries where, for example, the local company was committed to using nationally produced products or government policies prohibited the importing of certain equipment. These obstacles were added to the normal resistance to change experienced by people who are being asked to do things differently. It took major interventions and negotiations conducted by the top echelons of the organization to implement this change, and it took years longer than anticipated, but it has subsequently proved well worth the effort.

---

A large consumer company made a fundamental change in its relationships with its key customers by placing computer terminals in customers' purchasing offices, expanding the networks between organizations, and relocating the sources of major decisions. After much negotiation, the manufacturer and the customers agreed on the new system. However, due to a lag in the manufacturing organization's ability to produce the hardware and software that were needed, the actual implementation took two years longer than predicted.

---

Kenneth Olsen, CEO of Digital Equipment Corporation, started a weekly electronic letter to employees around the world. Each week he sent this letter, which could be read at the convenience of the local viewer. Questions and comments could be sent by electronic mail and Olsen responded to them in a subsequent letter. This type of system-wide information sharing will become common practice in the global organization of the nineties.

The Royal Bank of Canada's main office had been located in Montreal. In the early eighties they split their head-quarters between Montreal and Toronto. Because of the need for top management to interact frequently, senior executives spent hours on company and commercial air-planes, flying back and forth in the Canadian winter, and spending a day of executive time to attend a two-hour meeting.

The information specialists were well aware of the potential of video conferencing, but found that many members of top management were resistant to relying on this method, for both morale and security reasons. Finally, the top managers became so frustrated that they demanded a solution to the problem.

Today in the Montreal headquarters and in the Toronto headquarters, there is a bank-owned video sys-tem. Direct "face-to-face" conferences are available be-tween these centers by merely calling and setting up a meeting. No technicians are present, and the executives can manage the machinery themselves.

All of these possibilities require that the information man-agement division change its basic thinking from technical to stra-tegic management. Members of this division need to think like top managers, producing options for the top and then support-ing them with the appropriate technologies.

## Financial Management

A consequence of many fundamental change decisions is a change in the role and functions of the financial staff. It is important for financial information to be managed closer to the source, and networks must be developed to make information available at several levels simultaneously. In addition, it may be neces-sary to overhaul the business planning process. The responsibil-

ities of the finance staff in advising the top leadership will need
to be reexamined. What should they monitor and control? And
if the budget process becomes a direct interaction between business heads and an executive board, what should be the role of
the financial staff?

We have witnessed several occasions where lack of attention to this issue has caused tremendous tensions between the
field and headquarters, mainly because they are operating from
different assumptions — the old way and the new way — with little discussion about the best way.

## Other Functional Staffs

Perhaps the most serious disturbances in any fundamental change
are to the staff members who head the various activities, such as
manufacturing and sales. The support activities such as personnel and public relations may also be significantly affected.

One of the difficulties in adjusting to the changed state
is the tendency to hang onto the traditional labels of "line" and
"staff." In most organizations these are dysfunctional descriptions, to say nothing of being obsolete. A better way to think
about roles is in terms of "performers" and "supporters." Depending on the tasks, some are performers while others support or implement. Anyone who has managed a matrix organization knows this. However, many key executives do not operate
on this principle, but prefer the old labels and meanings.

Another consequence of this type of change is the necessity for collaboration between groups, which previously may
have been optional. If a product supply concept or a total quality program is introduced, all sorts of organizations must work
as a team to achieve results. If a team is defined as a group in
which all the members must have access to each other's resources
in order for the work to be done, then team operation will increase significantly as these major changes are implemented.

## Organizational Structure and Design

Any major change has implications for the way the organization is structured, the way the work flows, and the organiza-

tion's information and communication patterns. Inevitably, there is a developmental progression in the lives of all organizations. They start with an idea and a few eager people doing everything. As an organization grows, it becomes necessary to organize by functions: some people buy, some make the product, some sell, and some count the money.

This form is appropriate as long as there are only a few products that are sold in limited markets. But as life gets more complicated, it becomes necessary to change to a market or product focus, resulting in a business-related, profit-centered organization where each subset contains all the functions. When this gets too cumbersome and the tasks too varied, the decisions become matrixed. Joint responsibility and accountability are essential. This requires reallocation of decisions and the etablishment of relationships according to tasks.

The final stage of development, which is necessary in a fundamental change, is the mixed mode. The organization is designed to be optimally organized for all of its different basic tasks. The organizational structure and role assignments that have been appropriate for operating the current system may be quite inappropriate for designing the future, and even more inappropriate for managing a massive change. As a result, it is necessary to design temporary systems and various other parallel structures, which are tailored to essential tasks that have nothing to do with running today's business.

Failure to attend to "form follows function" management can result in mismatches, misalignments of effort, and inordinate attention being paid to relationships instead of to work. Changes in strategic priorities such as moving to a customer-driven stance from a technology-driven one require major reexamination of both decision and communication patterns, as well as of performance and promotion patterns.

## Rewards

A major factor affecting the success of any fundamental change is the establishment of consistency between the stated goals and priorities and the reward system that defines what is valued in the organization. Examples abound of situations where the official

statement of goals and priorities is inconsistent with the organization's practices.

---

One of us was a faculty member for a number of years
at the Sloan School of Management at Massachusetts Institute of Technology, a prestigious institution with its fair
share of Nobel laureates and distinguished scholars and
a "top-flight" school from which to graduate.

The stated purpose in all the brochures sent to
potential students was that the school was dedicated to
providing a first-class education in the management field.
There would be an opportunity to "rub minds" with outstanding scholars and to be taught by the best of them.

In fact, for a five-year period that we monitored,
the faculty member who won the "best teacher" award
from the students failed to get tenure. Why? Mainly because the senior faculty were primarily researchers, who
were not particularly interested in teaching. Their criteria
for promotion were heavily skewed toward the research
contributed by young faculty members, a fact that was
quickly learned by junior faculty members who wanted
to succeed in the system. They would join the faculty with
a great desire to teach. The senior faculty would let them—
it saved the tenured faculty members from doing it. But
when evaluation time came, it was the research, not the
teaching, on which the candidate was judged.

---

Unfortunately this condition is not unique to the Sloan
School. Nor is it relevant only in academia. Perhaps the most
common mismatch in business organizations is when the policy
is to encourage risk taking and innovation, but the rewards are
given for economic results and meeting business goals. Examples of consistent reward systems are, however, increasing as
more and more chief executives see the necessity of "putting the
company's money where the leaders' mouths are."

A good example of an aligned policy and reward system is that of the 3M Company.

---

The strategy at 3M is to bring new innovations on-stream at greater than the normal competitive speed. In this reward system, if a person "invents" an idea that is deemed worth pursuing by one or two people in the hierarchy above the inventor, a contract is drawn up in which the company creates a joint venture with him or her. The inventor shares in the profits as the product begins to produce revenue. This profit sharing is in addition to her or his regular compensation.

---

Incentive compensation is an area where alignment and nonalignment can make a great difference in employee motivation. Questions that need to be addressed include:

- What criteria should be used for allocating bonuses: company performance, unit performance, or personal performance?
- What should the weighting be for each of these?
- If there are performance-related discretionary payouts, who should allocate them: the unit head, the central personnel department, or top management?

---

An example of the possible complications that can arise from incentive compensation programs can be found in a large consumer products company that made a basic change in its values. Its governing factor, which had been increases in sales, had changed to profits. To underscore the importance of this change, the company developed an incentive compensation program that allowed those who produced profits to receive significant bonuses based on their performance. Unfortunately, the jobs of many members of the staff were not intended to bring in money—instead, they cost money.

The whole support side of the organization now was faced with an irrelevant bonus system. The management attempted to introduce a related system for them, but it was a makeshift policy. If management's intention was to increase motivation and commitment, it partially succeeded, but at a significant cost to the organization.

---

A further example illustrates the need for a consistent reward system.

---

The food division of a consumer company produced various prepared food products. Dog food, cat food, and cereals made up the product line. The division had been organized to take advantage of marketing opportunities such as securing shelf space in stores. Each of the businesses was a profit center, which competed for shelf space in the stores with all the other divisions of the company and whose advertising budget was managed by the division manager.

The company's compensation system paid large bonuses based mostly on company performance. The basic pay was on the low side for the industry. However, a person could more than double his or her base salary if company results were good. The allocation and distribution of bonuses to the executives of a division was the prerogative of the president of that division.

The president of the food group was extremely frustrated. He had initiated a series of Monday morning meetings of the division managers, the purpose of which was to identify and develop strategies for business issues that could benefit every profit center. For example, if each center contributed a portion of its advertising dollars to a corporate program that sponsored a major sporting event, the whole group would benefit. No single business could afford the costs by itself.

Attendance at these meetings was casual, to put it mildly. Members often had other business priorities that had to be taken care of that day, secretaries would bring in messages, and members would depart for an hour or so.

Another frustration felt by the president was the lack of activity on the part of the division managers in personally leading the career development and succession planning practices in their areas. The personnel department was constantly hounding the president, who was pushing the division managers, but the results were miserable.

One year, when bonus time came around, he called his key managers together and explained the basis for the bonus allocation that year. Sixty-five percent would be based on their business results, 25 percent would be based on his opinion of their contribution to the strategic planning for the group, and 10 percent would be based on his and the personnel department's evaluation of their performance in the area of development.

The following Monday the meeting was an amazing sight. Everyone was there, everyone contributed, good ideas emerged—it was a completely different group!

---

There is probably no single action management can take that will affect credibility more than making sure that the organization's strategies, policies, and pay, as well as more informal rewards and signals, are in conformity with each other.

# 7

■

# Leading the Transition: Strategies for Process, Commitment, and Communication

## The Transitional State

In all change, regardless of size and complexity, there are three states: the future state, when the change has been completed and the goals of the change have been achieved; the present state, or the current conditions; and the transitional state, the period of time in which all the change takes place.

Most senior managers are comfortable with defining goals and creating strategies to achieve them. Far fewer managers are aware of the need to manage the process of change. Many strategic plans die because of lack of implementation. There is a high correlation between the failure to implement changes and the lack of conscious management of the transitional process.

There are several activities that must be managed in a major change effort:

- Defining the tasks to be done
- Creating management structures dedicated to accomplishing these tasks
- Developing strategies for obtaining necessary commitment from key players

69

- Designing a strategy and mechanisms for the communication of the change
- Assigning dedicated resources, experts, and consultants to assist in managing the change

## Choices for Top Management Behavior

Leaders must continually determine their personal behavior. In any major activity they must choose which tasks they will *do* themselves, which tasks they will personally *manage,* and which tasks they will set up structures and allocate resources to manage — where they are *managing the management.* In a fundamental change effort, these choices are critical to the success of the effort. What processes are involved in making and implementing these choices?

## Managing the Work: Tasks and Activities

The transitional state — when all the change takes place — is unique in that it is neither the same as the present state nor identical with the changed state. The tasks to be done must be specific to the context in which they are done; therefore, the top leadership needs to define what has to be done, how it must be done, and who should do it.

### Identifying Tasks

In a fundamental change effort, the tasks are likely to include:

- A detailed study of the present conditions
- Collection of data on the attitudes of the organization's members toward the change
- Creation of models of the desired state
- Identification of and planning for a transitional management
- Assignment of functions to the transitional management
- A formal statement of the change goals and a clear description of the end state
- Identification and allocation of dedicated resources, experts, and consultants

It is in this phase — task identification — that top managers must personally do the work themselves. Most of the tasks we define cannot be delegated to other managers. Top management should, however, use special resources if needed.

One additional task that requires top management involvement is the preliminary sequencing of the tasks.

## Creating Management Structures

Creating structures to manage the transition is usually only possible by top management and is thus "managing the management."

The management paradigms and style of the chief executive usually determine how transitional management structures are set up. We believe that the optimum organizational design is based on the concept that form follows function and that management structures that allocate resources from across the organization are needed. Knowledge and experience will be the principal criteria for this allocation; organizational position will be less critical.

To illustrate this point, let us look at the decision to build a new plant.

---

### An Example of an Incremental Change Strategy

Top management decides a new plant should be built. The end state is an efficiently functioning plant characterized by low costs and high quality. To achieve this result, top management develops the list of tasks, identifies the sequencing of the tasks, and allocates the resources appropriate for each stage in the sequence. The real estate department acquires an appropriate site. The engineering department designs the building and its contents, including machines, offices, warehouses, and support facilities.

As the project continues, information specialists are added to the startup management. Financial specialists join the project. Personnel assigns recruiters and planners to develop policies consistent with the larger organization.

As the plant nears completion, the plant manager joins the process. From here on, the process changes from design to operations. The plant manager plays the key role in this transition.

---

In practice, no well-managed, effective organization would start up a plant in this manner. A more effective process would emerge from a fundamental change strategy.

---

### An Example of a Fundamental Change Strategy

If top management were to adopt a fundamental change strategy before allocating specific resources, it would first identify the future state—the plant in operation—and then create a plant (or works) startup team.

This team would be composed of the plant manager and dedicated resources from engineering, information management, personnel, and finance. The team's first assignment would be to design the work flow, the social structure, the personnel policies and practices, the financial systems and controls, and the interfaces (for example, between plant and warehouse managers).

The team's second assignment would be to determine the tasks and structures needed to get from the present condition to the plant in operation. The team would start from the image of the operating plant and ask the following questions: what values and assumptions will drive the effort? what communications, feedback practices, and individual and group development activities will be employed? what will the career development and succession planning procedures be?

The startup team would also identify what training would be required at what points. Team members would determine appropriate reporting procedures. They

would identify the relationship of the startup team with
the manufacturing management and with functions such
as purchasing, engineering, and distribution.

Top management's role in this process would have
been to:

- Create the management's structure—the startup team
- Define its tasks and relationships
- Define the expected outcomes from its work
- Define its "life expectancy"

---

## *Options for Management Structures*

There are several choices in defining the transitional management structure. In the situation we just described, top management could have chosen to set up a steering group to manage
the activities. Other options available for transitional management include:

- Top management (in this example, manufacturing management) could become the project managers.
- Top managers could appoint a "czar" or project leader.
- The change could be managed by creating a special change
  management team of specialists or staff.

There are additional options that can be used in any
change effort. In a fundamental change, it may well be necessary for top management to set up multiple managements to
direct various parts of the program.

In some of the massive change programs currently in
progress in Europe and America, leaderships have created steering groups for overall management. These groups have then
identified and put in place other groups, such as study groups,
and subgoal transitional managements.

## Developing Commitment Strategies

Organization leaders rarely think of obtaining commitment as
a part of the change process or as a condition that requires

strategy and implementation. Conventional wisdom sees resistance to change as a nuisance that must be overcome for the action goals to be achieved. We suggest that getting the commitment necessary to carry out organizational change requires the same type of analysis and planning as does the change itself.

## Managing Resistance to Change

In addition to the universal condition of the three states of change, there is a universal condition that wherever there is a change effort, there will be resistance. It may be caused situationally by the need to learn new things or destroy old and familiar ones, or it may result from the individual dynamics of a fear of failing, or of looking silly or incompetent. A dramatic illustration of the latter cause is seen in the difficulty of introducing computer terminals in executives' offices. Behind the "rational" resistances is usually the idea that "men don't type, senior executives don't do things clumsily, and they don't appear publicly until they are master of whatever they are doing."

In the types of changes we are discussing, resistance is likely to be found in the middle levels of senior management. Fear of loss of power is the obvious explanation, but equally possible is fear of not having enough to do, of boredom, or of uselessness.

Another location of resistance is farther down in the organization. In many situations the relevance of the change to the "world of work" decreases as it moves down the system. A change in ownership or marketing strategy in a big hotel is not likely to be felt by the headwaiter or executive housekeeper in any significant way. Their resistance to becoming excited about the change is often misinterpreted by those higher up and labeled as a lack of loyalty or as laziness.

The reaction to resistance often is anger and frustration. Those who resist are the "bad guys," so the energy goes into straightening them out, rather than finding the cause of the resistance and dealing with it in a nonjudgmental manner. Resistance is energy. Energy is the asset that drives the organizational machine. Resistance usually appears as negative energy, and that induces negative energy in management's dealings with it. Or, as often occurs, management's strategy is to get rid of the negative energy, to smooth things over. The net result of such a strategy is that the energy is reduced, and with it the asset that drives the system.

An effective strategy is one where the goal is to convert the negative energy to positive energy, to change the balance. Creating and stating clear goals, sharing the change strategy, appreciating contributions at all levels, and rewarding group progress are the types of action plans that tend to produce the best results.

A useful formula (from Beckhard and Harris, 1987) for thinking about the resistance process is:

$$C = (A + B + D) > X$$

where

$C$ = change
$A$ = level of dissatisfaction with the status quo
$B$ = desirability of the proposed change or end state
$D$ = practicality of the change (minimal risk and disruption)
$X$ = "cost" of changing

Factors $A$, $B$, and $D$ must outweigh the perceived costs $(X)$ for change to occur. If any person or group whose commitment is needed is not sufficiently dissatisfied with the present state of affairs $(A)$, eager to achieve the proposed end state $(B)$, and convinced of the feasibility of the change $(D)$, then the cost $(X)$ of changing is too high, and that person or group will resist the change.

Looking at the readiness for the change of key individuals whose commitment is needed against the dimensions of the formula can give some clues to the leaders about which strategies might be effective in reducing resistance and building commitment to change. For example, do the key players share a vision of the future possibilities? Can they be inspired or involved more in building and owning this vision? Or are they still satisfied with today's realities? Can they be convinced through evidence and persuasion that today's situation needs to change?

Or perhaps they are both committed to the new possibilities and dissatisfied with the status quo but do not know how to move forward. Can they be helped to see some possible first steps for moving forward with which they can be comfortable?

The morale in the organization, the atmosphere, and the attitudes of staff always have an impact on the productivity and quality of the organization's output. Nowhere is this more true than in times of major change. The inevitable ambiguity, confusion about tasks and authority, and apparently contradictory messages almost guarantee a short-term drop in morale, and perhaps in motivation. Most of us prefer some order in our lives. When this is removed, we consciously or unconsciously struggle to replace it with a new order. A strong natural tendency to resist change is an inevitable part of the process.

---

In 1990, the British Broadcasting Corporation aired a program called "The Troubleshooter" with Sir John Harvey-Jones, the business executive and recent chairman of Imperial Chemical Industries. Functioning as a consultant, Harvey-Jones would visit a company, analyze its condition, and make recommendations for improving effectiveness and results.

One such visit was to the Morgan car company, a maker of handmade automobiles with a worldwide reputation for quality. This was a family-owned business, with most of the employees having been with the firm for over thirty years. The company's product was excellent, its profit was mediocre, and its manufacturing methods were archaic. Harvey-Jones pointed out again and again that the quality of a handmade car could be maintained just as well with an electric screwdriver or drill as with a hand tool. This suggestion was met with massive resistance by both the owners and the workers. They had been making cars one way for years, the cars were excellent, and any change, even if it increased output with no loss of quality, was unacceptable. They were dug in.

---

This example of resistance might seem extreme, but it is not. The same level of resistance can occur in any organization trying to "destroy" old ways and replace them with new ones. Change, by nature, is destructive. It destroys the known and replaces it with the unknown, which someone thinks will be better. Many of those who are affected would prefer the "devil they know."

Poor morale and negative energy may not show up immediately after a change. Management may be lulled into thinking that everything is all right only to face an eruption, or at least a disruption, as the level of anxiety and anger increases, with consequent costs to productivity and morale.

A preemptive strategy can minimize this risk. From the outset, a communication plan is needed to pass information down, and all levels of management must institute a feedback process in their units, to become aware of staff attitudes.

### Developing a Critical Mass

A critical mass may or may not include all the members of a particular level or constituency. Instead, it is defined as the smallest number of people and/or groups who must be committed to a change for it to occur. Determination of what constitutes a critical mass requires an analysis of the formal organization, surrounding key constituencies, and their relevance to and position toward the change. From such an analysis a new system emerges that is smaller than the core system. This new system is composed only of those individuals and groups who are part of the critical mass.

A related process is the determination of the minimum commitment required from each player or group in order to allow the change to happen. The goal is not to achieve total commitment from everyone, but rather to obtain the minimum commitment necessary for success.

A way of thinking about this question has been developed that many managers have found helpful. Keeping in mind the desire to achieve the minimum commitment that is necessary, we can ask what we need of each member of the critical mass to accomplish the change. Do we need them to

- Make it happen?
- Help it happen, by providing resources?
- Let it happen, by not blocking the process?

To facilitate this analysis, a useful device called a "*commitment* chart" has been developed (see Figure 7.1). To create a chart, you first make a simple grid. Along the horizontal axis you draw four columns headed "Against," "Let," "Help," and "Make." On the vertical axis you list all the players, both individuals and groups, who make up the critical mass.

You then determine the necessary level of commitment for each player and mark an "O" in the appropriate box. For example, if the division managers have to "help it happen," you would indicate this with an "O." After locating the "desired state" for a player, you then locate his or her present state—for example, the division managers would generally be in the "let it happen" mode—and mark the box with an "X."

You then connect with an arrow the present position, X, with the required position, O. This tells you what has to be done

**Figure 7.1. Commitment Chart.**

| Key Players | No Commitment | Let It Happen | Help It Happen | Make It Happen |
|---|---|---|---|---|
| 1. | | X ——————— | —————→ O | |
| 2. | | X ——→ O | | |
| 3. | | X ——————— | —————→ O | |
| 4. | | O ←——— X | | |
| 5. | | | (XO) | |
| 6. | X ——→ O | | | |
| 7. | | X ——————— | —————→ O | |
| 8. | | (XO) | | |
| 9. | X ——————— | —————→ O | | |
| 10. | | | O ←——— X | |

*Source:* Beckhard and Harris, 1987. Used by permission.

to move everyone to the required position. When an X and an O are in the same box, you have the desired commitment. If they are not in the same box, you have to develop a strategy for getting them there.

## Developing a Commitment Plan

Once it is clear what is required to obtain needed commitment, action plans must be made and implemented. It may be that some strategies can be developed that will achieve the desired result from several players. On the other hand, it may be necessary to use different strategies for different players. Sometimes the necessary commitment can be obtained through the direct use of positional or other power. Sometimes a political strategy is appropriate.

If neither of these approaches is workable, other options are needed. We turn again to Beckhard and Harris (1987) for a description of some of these options.

### Problem Finding

Problem finding is [a] mechanism by which those concerned with change get together to identify and clarify all aspects of the problem. Problem finding allows players to change their minds without having to say so. It also allows people to listen to each other — temporarily — without having to screen what they hear through their own biases. It assumes that the very process of clarifying an issue or problem, as opposed to problem solving or action taking, will be unthreatening enough to encourage commitment.

There are several important rules to remember in problem finding, all of them aimed at limiting the sense of risk among the participants:

- It must be bounded. The activity can only be for the purpose of problem and issue identification; no action is allowed.

- It must have a minimum of structure. There must be a clear willingness to limit the work to clarification, but within that framework the exchange of ideas would be as free as possible.
- It must have a minimum of public output. There need be no minutes, and certainly no public statement of consensus or agreement.
- It must be temporary. An ad hoc requirement is important.

## Educational Intervention

Just as problem-finding activities are designed to unfreeze attitudes, so are educational interventions. The concept here is that there are two places inside which the activities of our daily lives are irrelevant: the house of worship and the school or, more broadly, the learning situation.

In the classroom, it usually does not matter who you are the rest of the time; all students are equal during class. For improving communication skills, it is irrelevant what students do in their professional and private lives; they are all here to learn.

Educational activities for managing organizational change can help people to understand a change problem and to offer needed commitment.

## Role Modeling

There are times when commitment can be achieved only if it is seen as required, or if the leaders "practice what they preach" by clearly demonstrating their own commitment to the change. One way of sending this message is for the norm setters (organization leaders) to change their personal behavior. The norm setters thus provide role models for other members of the organization, demonstrating that "this change activity has priority; it is as relevant as our operating responsibilities."

## Changing Rewards

A powerful way of reinforcing a change in priorities is to change the reward system. Too often, organizations encourage resistance by maintaining a reward system that is inconsistent with the new state of affairs. For example, if you want your employees to be more innovative, but you maintain a financial reward system and an appraisal procedure that only reward concrete results of meeting quotas (thus implicitly punishing "mavericks"), do not be surprised to find a fairly high resistance to innovation, and a credibility problem to boot.

The current literature is full of illustrations of the impact of changing reward systems. More and more companies are attaching rewards to the output of ideas or participation in improvement ideas. For example, the 3M reward system for innovative ideas has significantly increased the creation of new and imaginative products in that organization.

The ideal reward system strives for a balance between rewards for what a person knows and for what he or she does. This system is out of balance in the hiring of graduates and master's degree students for industry, because they are rewarded much less for what they do than for what they know in their initial jobs. Conversely, in traditional manufacturing organizations, people in the workplace are rewarded disproportionately for what they do, and very little for what they know. Most new plants and organizations that are trying to develop [a] better quality of work and working life are changing the reward system to one in which there is a better balance between the value of what a person knows and the value of what he or she does.

## Responsibility Allocation

It is often necessary to develop some low-risk mechanism or activity that allows people to collaborate even if they have vastly different biases. This only works, however, when there is already consensus on a bigger objective, within which disagreements over lesser issues can be explored.

Much change takes place at the interface between departments, between merging organizations, and through internal reorganization. Wherever the change brings the units of a larger whole into a new or different relationship, such questions arise as: "Who should act upon whom?" or "How should each party behave under the changed circumstances?" Traditional ways of dealing with this issue are:

*Write new job descriptions.* This approach makes the assumption that the conditions of and relationships between job roles are always the same regardless of the tasks to be done. The reality is that tasks change and location of authority shifts depending on the tasks. For example, under one condition manufacturing staff might be the "performers" and marketing personnel the "supporters," whereas in other circumstances it might be exactly the opposite.

*Let the boss decide.* Bosses are usually chosen as decision makers because of their higher position in the power structure—not because they have more information than the subordinates. Letting the boss decide is a waste of management time and energy, because if an organization is trying to push decisions down to the lowest level where sufficient information occurs, having bosses mediate issues between two subordinates does not add any information to the situation but involves a third party simply on the basis of power.

*Applying the "expert" solution.* Consultants or experts provide the "proven" solution. This can often provide useful guidelines; but the expert solution that may work in one place doesn't necessarily apply in another place or another situation.

All three of these alternatives operate from the standpoint of defining the "roles" of interacting parties. A more productive way of approaching the problem, we believe, is to find out the behavior desired. To do this, one needs to define the optimum behavior for each of the several roles that affect a particular decision or action.

## Responsibility Charting

A technique called *responsibility charting* (Beckhard and Harris, 1987) has been developed to assess alternative behaviors related to different decisions. Responsibility charting clarifies the behavior that is required to implement important change tasks, actions, or decisions.

In the basic process, two or more people whose roles interrelate or who manage interdependent groups formulate a list of actions, decisions, or activities that affect their relationship (such as developing budgets, allocating resources, and deciding on the use of capital) and record the list on the vertical axis of a responsibility chart (see Figure 7.2). They then identify the people involved in each action or decision and list these "actors" on the horizontal axis of the form. Actors can include:

- The individuals who are directly involved in a decision
- The bosses of those involved
- Groups (boards of directors, project teams)
- People outside of the organization (union officials, auditors, bankers)

Finally, the participants chart the appropriate behavior of each actor with regard to any particular action or decision, using the following classifications:

R       Has *responsibility* for a particular action, but not necessarily authority

A       Must *approve*—has the power to veto the action

**Figure 7.2. Responsibility Chart.**

| Actors / Decisions or Acts | | | | | | | | | | | | | | | | |
|---|---|---|---|---|---|---|---|---|---|---|---|---|---|---|---|---|
| | | | | | | | | | | | | | | | | |
| | | | | | | | | | | | | | | | | |
| | | | | | | | | | | | | | | | | |
| | | | | | | | | | | | | | | | | |
| | | | | | | | | | | | | | | | | |
| | | | | | | | | | | | | | | | | |
| | | | | | | | | | | | | | | | | |

R = Responsibility (not necessarily authority)
A = Approval (right to veto)
S = Support (put resources toward action)
I = Informed (to be consulted before action)
– = Irrelevant to this item

*Source:* Beckhard and Harris, 1987. Used by permission.

S Must *support*—has to provide resources for the action (but not necessarily agree with it)

I Must be *informed or consulted* before the action, but cannot veto it

— Irrelevant to the action

## Designing Communication Strategies and Mechanisms

In a fundamental change effort, the normal communication procedures and practices will not be adequate or even appropriate. Top management should see that a communication plan and process that are dedicated to supporting the change effort are created and monitored. This may well mean assigning resources to the effort and using, for example, new information networks or special channels. Creative use of closed-circuit television, teleconferences, and computer conferencing can assure significantly better motivation as well as understanding.

The amount of effort that can successfully be put into communication is often underestimated. As well as providing people with information, communication is an essential prerequisite to changing attitudes and behavior, ways of work, relationships, and so on, all of which are likely to be necessary to fundamental change.

*Passive communication* is the type of communication most often used to inform people in an organization about changes that are being made or are to be made. This is substantially one-way (downward) communication, and although it may engage people intellectually, it does not necessarily result in any emotional commitment. People also forget, and sometimes they do not hear what they have been told. Messages that are very familiar to top management must be repeated and repeated, more than top management would believe to be necessary.

---

In one division of an international company that was making major changes to its strategy, structure, and culture in a massive effort to improve its business performance, the top management held a big meeting with key staff to describe what was happening, to outline its vision for the future, and to provide some motivation and direction. During later opinion surveys the majority of the people who attended said that they did not know what the vision was and insisted that they had never heard it. As it turned out, what was in most people's minds during this talk from top management was the question: "Will I have a job?" Therefore, the message about an optimistic and exciting vision of the future was never heard. This was a salutary lesson for the members of top management who believed that they had communicated their message.

---

Finding some way of measuring the gap between the messages sent by top management and those received by the intended audience is critical in an effective change process. Targeted employee opinion surveys can be a very valuable way for top management to receive feedback about this and other aspects of change.

*Active communication* can be a very powerful adjunct to more traditional downward communication and plays a key part in helping to make change happen. In active communication, the communication process is designed so that people become involved with it personally and begin to translate the messages into the question: "What does this mean for me, my behavior, my way of working, my relationships, and so on?" In addition, people engage with the subjects emotionally as well as intellectually. Without this process, there is likely to be little change or commitment. Building understanding and ownership are crucial parts of a communication strategy and should be designed as learning processes for the organization.

---

An active communication process was used when Statoil communicated its "Vision 2000" to its top fifty managers. Part of the meeting was input from the president and his colleagues on the work the top group had done; the fifty managers then met in smaller groups to address specific questions that would provide feedback to the top management and, in the process, engage the fifty managers in actively thinking together about the direction of the company and the actions they should be taking to help it reach its goal.

---

---

A global company created a newsletter that was transmitted weekly by electronic mail to employees throughout the world. The purpose of the change was reiterated, the major activities were identified, and subchanges were reported. "Crunches" and "watchouts" were also identified. The management credits this communication plan with

making a significant difference in the smoothness with
which the change plan was implemented.

---

## Recruiting and Using Dedicated Expertise

In addition to the use of study groups, transition teams, and
so forth, there will probably be a need for some specialists—
both inside and outside the organization—to be dedicated to
the change on a part-time or full-time basis.

Contributions may be made by experts in information
technology or strategic planning, economists and financial strat-
egists, organizational consultants, counselors, and training specialists. We would like to suggest some questions chief executives might ask in order to decide what resources may be needed
for specific purposes, how they should function, and how long
they should be retained:

- What types of expertise will we require?
- Are experts available inside the system?
- Can they function effectively from within the system?
- If not, what outside expertise is required?
- How important is the chemistry between the expert and
  clients?
- What would be a "best fit" and how do we ensure it?
- What will we require from the resource: expert solutions,
  expert advice, consultation, training or education, techni-
  cal help, transfer of skills, or development of our capability?
- For how long will we require expert help?
- What type of contract would be optimal?
- What will this require of our personal behavior?
- How will we integrate the efforts of different types of help?

### Choosing Resource Help

It is important and all too seldom done to think through the
type of assistance required and to use the answers to the above
questions as a guide in selecting help, particularly from out-

siders. Each specialist brings to the engagement her or his own biases and ways of thinking. If the client is not clear about what is wanted, the expert may decide the content of the change and how it will be managed. These decisions should be retained by the change management.

For example, if background on the environment or on future macroeconomic forecasts is needed, economists will probably have to be retained. They may be tempted to advise management on what ought to be done in the future. This advice may be helpful, but it should be treated as just that, advice, and not as if it were binding on the organization's actions.

Advice and guidance on redesigning the organization to fit new requirements may be needed, including recommendations on structure, staffing, communication patterns, or information flow. It is important to decide whether recommendations or action plans should involve interviewing numbers of people, fitting them into frameworks, and then suggesting a course of action. Many strategic planning consultants follow this format and it may be just the type of help that is needed. This can be an "instrumental" approach, in which the consultants give expert answers or recommendations.

On the other hand, consultation that will help the organization to think through consequences and develop options on its own may well call for a different type of consultant. Organizational consultants and some organization development specialists are appropriate in this situation. If, as we have discussed in earlier chapters, the organization is aiming to become a "learning organization," it is important to think about any help that may be hired in relation to what will help the organization to accelerate its learning and develop its skills.

---

When a large global company decided to change its relationship with its key customers to allow them to have direct access to areas such as inventory control and ordering, they needed expert help to determine the best software and hardware to support the effort.

They did not realize until the effort was well under way, and a large number of organizational problems surfaced, that they also needed expert help in managing the process of introducing these changes.

Another dilemma is whether the primary need is for expertise in the content or technology — providing answers — or for consultation on how to go about approaching an issue, where the expertise on process is more important than on specific answers or content. One way of thinking about this is to ask whether a one-time solution is what is needed. In that case, expertise on content is probably the better choice. If the situation is repetitive or if it is best to develop the expertise internally, consulting help with a process or developmental orientation will be needed.

As a result of massive changes in the functioning of the National Health Service in Great Britain, many new types of work relationships, rewards, and skills were required. Many of the leaders were not very sophisticated in managing change. They both needed and asked for assistance. Initial efforts to bring in outside expertise were sufficient for early activities, but it soon became apparent that a much larger number of resources would be needed. A program was started to train change facilitators from among the managerial ranks of the Service so that this expertise would be available. External consultants were used to help design and develop this process of growing internal expertise.

A large company undertook a massive change effort to optimize its work and working conditions. Thousands of employees who had worked in a relatively structured hierarchy were now going to work in a collaborative mode. Among other major interventions was one where every

working unit determined the criteria against which the performance of the unit should be measured, then assessed
where they were now on each criterion and where they
would like to be a year from now.

Managing this vast activity took team management,
change management, and conflict management skills,
which many managers did not have. A four-week course
was developed to train "change agents" to provide consultation to unit heads, and within a three-month period
there were skilled resources in each division so that managers could call on "local expertise" to help both in the
management of the project and in skill acquisition.

---

## Managing the Experts

Complex change efforts often require a number of different types
of expertise and consultation. Most often, the various experts
and their clients are treated autonomously with little regard for
synergy or collaboration. Opportunities for innovative and creative programs become buried in parallel arrangements.

In the same way that it is important for leaders to maintain an integrated perspective on the constellation of interconnected changes that makes up any fundamental change, it is
also important to manage in an integrated way any help that
may be hired for these changes. Many organizational leaders,
recognizing this, are now explicitly creating a process for managing these resources. In several companies we know, one particular person or role has the assignment of managing and acting
as liaison with all organizational and management consultants.
Such a person may convene consultants' meetings on a periodic basis for exchanges of ideas, interaction with top management, perspective sessions, and professional development. One
of the better examples of this practice took place in TRW Systems.

---

TRW Systems recruited six outside consultants, who met
with a similar number of human resource managers three

times a year for several days as a change team. The synergy that resulted and their ability to coordinate changes and cope with surprises was a tribute to the organization's capacity to harness team effort, energy, and creativity. A bottom-line result was that frequently delivery of a quality product took place on or before deadline with a financial bonus as a direct corollary.

---

## Defining the Relationship — The Contract Setting

There are a number of issues to consider after choosing the resource.

*Setting the Ground Rules.* Unless the client takes the lead in collaboratively setting the ground rules, they will be set by the resource or by accident, neither of which is desirable. Agreeing early on rules and guidelines will save a lot of grief later.

*Determining Access.* The client should participate in deciding on the consultants' access to various parts of the organization. The client should be satisfied that value can be added from the consultants' contact with selected individuals and groups.

Remember that this contact in itself is an intervention. Unless the ground rules are agreed upon and made clear, people will ask, "Why are they here?" "What will be done with the data that are collected?" "Who are they spying for?" It is wise to discuss this and reach agreement early.

*Determining Intervention Strategies.* Again, this should be a collaborative process. If the key management is not committed to owning the intervention strategy, its probability of success will be low and the likelihood of problems will be high. It is essential that the strategy be the leaders and that the resource be in a support role. This does not mean that the consultant may not be extremely visible from time to time, giving lectures, leading a segment of work, or ensuring quality control. It does mean that the management of the effort should be controlled by the management of the organization.

Connected to this is the need for early discussion about the probable consequences of various strategies and for thought about how these will or might be handled.

*Timetables and the Sequence of Activities.* It is always a good practice to agree on these elements in advance with the flexibility to modify them as events dictate.

*Resourcing.* Staffing of special resources, budgeting for their help, observing their performance, and periodically reviewing the relationship should all be part of the contract setting.

*Communicating the Roles and Functions of Experts to the Organization.* It is desirable to develop a plan for communicating information, to those who should have it, about the functions of the resources, their relationship to relevant parts of the organization, and what the rules about decisions, authority, and reporting relationships are.

### Summary

In an effective change effort — particularly when a fundamental change is required — it is critical for top management to pay attention to the process of change and transition, in addition to leading the change itself.

The organizational leaders must be sensitive to several aspects of the transition: managing the work; developing structures appropriate for and dedicated to managing specific tasks and activities; devising strategies and plans for ensuring the commitment of key players to the change goals and their personal involvement in achieving them; creating a communications strategy specifically designed to support the change goals and program; and deploying dedicated special expertise to help manage the transitional process.

Management needs to determine which of these aspects it will personally manage, and for which it will deploy and monitor their management.

Good choices will help ensure top-class business outcomes and significant increases in the organization's ability to be the best.

# 8

---
■
---

# Epilogue:
# Visionary Leaders and
# Transformed Organizations

## Conditions in the Next Decade

The predictable conditions of the transitional decade of the 1990s, including the unpredictability of events, will require more fundamental change efforts involving large organizations than at any time in the past.

We live at a time in history when the basic institutions of society and the relationships between them are being reevaluated and redesigned. The role of wealth production in the society and the allocation of wealth between rich and poor, the First and Third Worlds, and north and south are taking new forms. The relationships between governments, the so-called nongovernmental sector composed of groups of volunteers and citizens, and the producers of goods and services—the private sector—are in constant change. Anyone in a leadership position in a large organization has to be acutely aware of these changes and the challenges that result from them.

Communication technology has transformed the planet into one world, whether we like it or not. In addition to the incredible changes in the political face of the world, we are witnessing new alliances and coalitions of values that have direct impact on those who produce the world's wealth. If consumers feel that a company's efficient quality product is being manufactured at the cost of significant environmental pollution, they may very well buy a less efficient, "healthier" product from a competitor. There is clear evidence that graduates, in choosing the company they would like to join, are putting significant weight on the perceived social agenda of the competing companies. This is a major change in priorities from that of the same type of population in the eighties.

Advances in information and communication technology mean that the locations of manufacturing and research functions will change. Those countries with many human resources in the development of technology are likely to focus more on researching, inventing, and creating new ideas, whereas less-developed countries with lower educational levels will become the centers of manufacturing and production.

## The Thriving Organization

Organization leaders who are committed to and active in designing the future of their organization can be certain of one fact: the environment will be increasingly uncertain. Predicting the future will be both difficult and challenging.

A paradox is that the more uncertain the environment, the more there is need for a well-designed and -managed organization that is purposeful and energized to thrive in such uncertainty. Such an organization will have a widely shared value that "we can and will create our own destiny!" All levels of the organization will be aligned with the top leadership in a vision of the future, strategies for achieving that vision, and redesigns of the organization's work and culture to implement the strategies. There will be a balance between managing current and short-term work and managing the profound changes required to ensure a positive future.

The character of the thriving organization will show through its behavior. Key behavioral traits are:

- A superior ability to sense signals in the environment
- A strong sense of purpose
- The ability to manage toward visions

- Widely shared knowledge of where the organization is going
- An open culture with open communications
- A commitment to being a learning organization, with policies and practices that support this stance
- Valuing data and using it for planning both results and improvement
- High respect for individual contributions
- High respect for team and group efforts
- Explicit — and continuing — recognition of innovative and creative ideas and actions
- High tolerance for different styles
- High tolerance for uncertainty
- Structures that are driven by tasks
- High correlation between corporate or group visions and unit goals and strategies
- Good alignment between business goals and plans and the organization's capacity to perform
- The ability to successfully resolve the tension between high performance and continual performance

### The Winning Leadership

The leadership of a thriving organization will see as one of its basic functions the creation of conditions that produce commitment and creative actions by the people in the organization. The leadership will also:

- Be committed to both top performance results and maximum learning and development.
- Establish reward systems that balance recognition for business results with recognition for improvement, initiative, and creativity.
- Think in systems terms.
- Be highly aware of the tensions between the environmental demands and the organization's business and organizational vision and goals.
- Consciously manage the tensions between business strategies and the organization's culture

- Behave in ways that address — at all levels — the tensions between organizational priorities and individual needs.
- Be risk takers, committed both to performance management and change management.
- Think strategically, not tactically.
- Be visionary, having a clear picture of its organization in the future.
- Think in process terms, as well as in actions.
- Be passionate about winning. It will be driven to be the best — the top competitor, the survivor.
- Be deeply committed to personal leadership of change programs consciously designed to create the organization's best future.

### Changing the Essence

As we said in the Preface, this book is addressed primarily to those who have the ultimate responsibility for guiding their organizations into the next century.

We raised many more questions than we provided answers. It is our hope that this book will be helpful to leaders as they develop their own answers and actions.

# References

Argyris, C., and Schön, D. A. *Organizational Learning: A Theory of Action Perspective.* Reading, Mass.: Addison-Wesley, 1978.

Beckhard, R., and Harris, R. T. *Organization Transitions: Managing Complex Change.* (2nd ed.) Reading, Mass.: Addison-Wesley, 1987.

de Geus, A. "Planning as Learning." *Harvard Business Review,* March/April 1988.

Harvey-Jones, Sir J. *Making It Happen: Reflections on Leadership.* London: Collins, 1988.

Harvey-Jones, Sir J. *Getting It Together.* London: Heinemann, 1991.

Kanter, R. M. *The Change Masters.* New York: Simon & Schuster, 1983.

Lorenz, C. *London Financial Times,* Jan. 9, 1991.

Olins, W. *Corporate Identity.* London: Thames and Hudson, 1989.

Schein, E. H. *Organization Psychology.* Englewood Cliffs, N.J.: Prentice-Hall, 1985.

Senge, P. *The Fifth Discipline.* New York: Doubleday, 1990.

Tichy, N. "Crotonville: A Staging Ground for Corporate Revolution." *The Executive,* 1989, *3.*

Watson, J. N., and Pritchard, W. A. "A Group in Transition." In A. Brackel (ed.), *People and Organizations Interacting.* New York: Wiley, 1985.

# Suggestions for Further Reading

Argyris, C. *Reasoning, Learning, and Action: Individual and Organizational.* San Francisco: Jossey-Bass, 1982.

Beer, M. *Organization Change and Development.* Santa Monica, Calif.: Goodyear, 1980.

Bennis, W. *On Becoming a Leader.* Reading, Mass.: Addison-Wesley, 1989.

Bushe, G. R. and Shani, A. B. *Parallel Learning Structures.* Reading, Mass.: Addison-Wesley, 1991.

Ciompo, D. *Total Quality.* Reading, Mass.: Addison-Wesley, 1991.

Cohen, B. D. *Influence Without Authority.* New York: Wiley, 1990.

De Pree, M. *Leadership Is an Art.* New York: Doubleday, 1989.

Drucker, P. F. *Innovation and Entrepreneurship.* New York: Harper-Collins, 1986.

Fritz, R. *The Path of Least Resistance.* New York: Fawcett-Columbine, 1989.

Gardner, J. *On Leadership.* New York: Free Press, 1989.

Hanna, D. P. *Designing Organizations for High Performance.* Reading, Mass.: Addison-Wesley, 1988.

Hirschorn, C. *Managing in the New Team Environment.* Reading, Mass.: Addison-Wesley, 1991.

Hornstein, H. A. *Managerial Courage.* New York: Wiley, 1986.

Kanter, R. M. and Stein, B. *The Tale of "O": On Being Different in an Organization.* New York: HarperCollins, 1986.

McGregor, D. *The Human Side of Management.* New York: McGraw-Hill, 1960.

Maslow, A. H. *Eupsychian Management.* Homewood, Ill.: Dow Jones-Irwin, 1965.

Mitroff, I. *Break-Away Thinking.* New York: Wiley, 1988.

Mohrman, S. A. and Cummings, T. G. *Self-Designing Organizations.* Reading, Mass.: Addison-Wesley, 1989.

Morgan, G. *Creative Organization Theory.* Newbury Park, Calif.: Sage, 1989.

Pettigrew, A. *The Awakening Giant.* Oxford: Basil Blackwell, 1986.

Renesch, J. (ed.) *New Traditions in Business.* San Francisco: New Leaders Press, 1991.

Schein, E. *Organizational Culture and Leadership: A Dynamic View.* San Francisco: Jossey-Bass, 1985.

Tichy, N. M. *Managing Strategic Change.* New York: Wiley, 1983.

Weisbord, M. *Productive Workplaces: Organizing and Managing for Dignity, Meaning, and Community.* San Francisco: Jossey-Bass, 1987.

# Index